LIBRARY OF CONGRESS CATALOGUE CARD NUMBER 61-11005/TYPOGRAPHY BY CHARLES H. FALK STUDIO/
LITHOGRAPHED BY AMERICAN PRINTING AND LITHOGRAPHING COMPANY/PUBLISHED BY ANGEL ISLAND
PUBLICATIONS, INC./COPYRIGHT 1961 BY WILLIAM H. RYAN, ALL RIGHTS RESERVED. FIRST PRINTING.

THE ARTISTS' & WRITERS' COOKBOOK

EDITED BY

BERYL BARR

AND

BARBARA TURNER SACHS

DESIGNED BY

NICOLAS SIDJAKOV

CONTACT

EDITIONS

SAUSALITO, CALIFORNIA

dedicated
to the art of imperfection
in the kitchen

TABLE OF CONTENTS

FOREWORD

When I was a very little girl I collected buttons. My mother gave me a lovely string of old buttons from her mother. When I was about fifteen years old I commenced collecting recipes. The first one was of family cookies. Though I knew painters and writers, they gave me no recipes. Much later, Francis Picabia gave me a recipe for oeufs Picabia which is now amongst butter recipes in Gourmet, without his name. It is an extravagant recipe: twelve eggs and a pound of butter are mixed over a very, very low flame in the cocotte in which they will be served. Keep turning with a fork while very slowly adding to the eggs in very small quantities the pound of butter, not a speck less, never allowing it to boil. It should take $\frac{1}{2}$ hour to prepare, and produce eggs of a very suave consistency. That is the only recipe that an artist or writer has ever given me.

When I saw the first drafts of this book I sat down with a magnifying glass — my sight is dim. What I deciphered filled me with an enthusiasm and a jealousy — I want to have written the book! It is an enchanting book. The writers write as they write, the painters write as they paint. It is an honor that a cook has been asked to write about them.

Among the fascinating recipes in this book are a few from artists and writers I have known: Jacques Lipchitz, who supervised a wonderful kitchen when he lived in Paris before the war, Man Ray, Robert Graves, Mark Tobey, Stanley William Hayter and Ralph Stackpole. When I knew Ralph Stackpole he lived on more conventional food, but his salade auvergnate is typically from the south of France — dandelions, walnut oil, white wine vinegar, garlic and two hard-boiled eggs, chopped.

But those who are the most romantic are those who have the simplest titles, as Isak Dinesen with oysters au naturel (presumably from her Danish, not her African experience) and James Merrill, than whose taste surely nothing can be more distinguished, contributing garlic soup. Marcel Duchamp, leaving surrealism behind, teaches the way to prepare what would be a commonplace dish for anyone else: boeuf tartare, which is not what I am being served at my maison de santé, but is agreeable and nourishing and not at all boresome.

Spareribs by Pearl Buck are only more Chinese than the Chinese with the over- and undertones of their sauces, the fragrance of their restaurants. Would Kay Boyle be cooking her ratatouille for her grandchildren? I like John Logan selecting a pizza to put in the oven for us. And dear Upton Sinclair, his life in rice, in everything he himself must eat.

Sybille Bedford has always held my attention. I met her in Rome, where I spent the winter, and she was as lively as ever. We ate great quantities of the homemade pâté de foie gras of our hostess. One of the best meals I ever ate was served under her direction at the home of one of our friends.

It was also in Rome this winter that I met Donald Downes, whose table was exceptional, even for Rome. His cookbook is fabulous and in Trastevere, where he has his flat, he has the most exquisite meals, prepared with infinite taste. He had been visiting with a friend in an 11th-century Saracen tower overlooking the Mediterranean and cooking local dishes provided by the visiting Druses. His recipe in this book is for a Druse method of cooking mutton.

Now, here are three "artists' and writers'" recipes which I give to you: one a Burgundian pastry which Gertrude Stein and I were once served, one a fillet of sole with lobster sauce, Carl van Vechten's great favorite, and the third, an omelet recipe which George Sand sent to Victor Hugo.

GOUGERE, A BURGUNDIAN PASTRY ♫ Fred Tenevery took Gertrude Stein and me to the Baronne Pierlot's home, where the Baronne suggested to Gertrude Stein that we should spend the day in her cellar, where they made the wine, as a quiet place to work. The lunch served there, by the Baronne Pierlot's son, always consisted of a large roast. It was usually preceded by an egg dish. One day we were served a Burgundian gougère. It was made very much like a cream puff. The recipe, which is said to have originated in Lens, France, is found not only in Burgundy, but also in Troyes in the province of Champagne, and in various other parts of France.

The dough: Put in a thick, flat-bottom casserole 1 cup of water, $\frac{1}{4}$ pound of butter and a teaspoonful of salt. As soon as the water comes to a boil, withdraw the casserole from the high flame and add 2 cups of sifted flour. Mix, dry out the dough over a high flame, working it with a wooden spoon (like pâté a chou) until well detached from the sides of the casserole. Then, removed from the fire, add 5 whole eggs, one by one, $\frac{1}{4}$ pound of Gruyère cheese cut into small cubes, and a pinch of white pepper.

The icing: Scoop into a soupspoon the above-described dough and form patties the size of an egg. Deposit these patties one after the other in a buttered baking dish, arranging them side-by-side in a circle. Adjust the circle both outside and in with the back of a spoon. Glaze with egg yolk, sprinkle with cheese cut in tiny cubes and bake in a slow oven.

Gougère is usually served cold, but can also be served hot as an hors d'oeuvre.

FILLET OF SOLE WITH LOBSTER SAUCE (CARL VAN VECHTEN'S FAVORITE) ℘ Wash the fillets of two soles weighing about ¾ pound each, reserving the rest of the fish—that is the heads, tails, fins and small side bones. Roll the fillets and skewer them. Bring to a boil in their juice 12 fine oysters. Remove from the fire and reserve the juice. Bring to a boil without water in a covered saucepan 1 quart of mussels. As soon as the shells open remove them from the heat. Remove the mussels from the shells, and reserve the juice. Cook, covered, in a small saucepan ½ pound fresh mushrooms in 1 tablespoon of butter, 1 tablespoon of water and 1 tablespoon of lemon juice. Boil for 10 minutes, reserve the juice. Now bring to a boil, covered, 1 medium carrot, 1 medium onion, a bouquet of 1 stalk of celery, 1 twig of thyme, 1 laurel leaf, 1 clove, 1 cup of dry white wine and 1 cup of water. Add salt and pepper, the heads, tails, and bones of the fish and the juice of the oysters, mussels, and mushrooms. Simmer for ½ hour. Remove from the heat and strain. This is a court bouillon.

Shell ½ pound of shrimps, put aside with the oysters, mussels and mushrooms. Put the court bouillon in a saucepan, cover, and bring to a boil. Put in the rolled fillets, simmer for 10 minutes. Put 3 tablespoons of butter in a saucepan, add 2 tablespoons crushed lobster eggs pounded through a fine sieve with a potato masher. Moisten with a little of the court bouillon, whip with a whisk. Stir the yolks of 3 eggs and add 1 cup of hot cream. Pour into the court bouillon over a low flame, stir, do not allow to boil. Add oysters, mussels, mushooms and shrimps. Add in very small quantities ¼ pound of butter. Do not stir but mix by tipping the saucepan in all directions. Remove from the flame, add a squeeze of lemon juice, and serve.

OMELETTE AURORE (SENT BY GEORGE SAND TO VICTOR HUGO) ℒ Beat 8 eggs with a pinch of salt, 1 tablespoon sugar and 3 tablespoons heavy cream. Prepare the omelet in the usual manner. Before folding it, place on it 1 cup diced candied fruit and small pieces of marrons glacés which have soaked for several hours in 2 tablespoons of curaçao. Fold the omelet to keep the fruit in place, on a fireproof serving dish. Surround with marrons glacés and candied cherries. Cover at once with frangipani cream made by stirring 2 whole eggs and 3 yolks with 3 tablespoons of sugar until they are pale lemon-colored. Then add 1 cup of flour and a pinch of salt, stirring until it is perfectly smooth. Add 2 cups of milk and mix well. Put the mixture in a saucepan over the lowest heat and stir until it is quite thick. It must not boil. Be careful that the cream does not become attached to the bottom or sides of the saucepan. When it has thickened remove it from the heat and add 2 tablespoons of butter and 3 powdered macaroons. Stir and mix well. Pour the sauce over the omelet and sprinkle ¼ cup diced angelica over the top. Then sprinkle 6 powdered macaroons on top and, finally, 3 tablespoons of melted butter. Place the omelet in a preheated 550-degree oven only long enough to brown it lightly.

Alice B. Toklas
Paris, France

APROPOS

1

SYBILLE BEDFORD 🍇 ON ABSOLUTE FOOD When the phylloxera — the American vine louse — was about to destroy the vineyards of the Médoc some eighty years ago, the vines were saved by grafting on American roots which were immune to the disease. Since then, the wines of Europe are made from native stock upon transatlantic roots. At the same time, the Pinot, the Cabernet, the Riesling, the Muscat and the Sauvignon, the classical grape varieties of France and Germany and Italy are grown and flourish, after another fashion, in California and the lakes of New York State. Food and wine, and the raising of food and wine, are at once the most and the least localized of the skills. Their development is due to commerce and to travel, and their continuity to stout regionalism; they take their character from the resources of the soil and climate at hand, yet may enrich it by an adaptation of some of the good things from outside.

And so in cookery every enlarging contribution was made by articulate and travelled men, yet the burden has been carried on by obscure local women. The history of cooking, if it were ever written, would be one of interchanges and migrations. Certain styles of cooking run like threads across the globe, and certain folk themes appear over and over again at places once unrelated to each other.

I see food in cycles. The older cycle of the Mediterranean and the East, of rice and beans, olive oil, garlic, the skewered lamb, the coruscating fish, melon and peaches. The temperate cycle of the well-tilled West, beef and butter, green vegetables, plump fowl, cream, a prodigality of cheeses, white bread, apples, berries. The poorer sunless cycle of the North, oatmeal and barley, root vegetables, herring and cod, lard and pig.

I have loved all food at its hour. From the chicken leg devoured in hand to the *suprême velouté* to the dish of boiled bacon and greens. But what I love most — now

2

—is an abundance of simple food of perfect quality and staggering freshness, very simply and very respectfully treated, tasting strongly of itself. *Absolute food* one might call it. The fish out of water, grilled by the sea shore, seasoned with lemon, sea salt, olive oil and perhaps a sprig of rosemary. The meat and the bird roasted over an open fire. The young vegetable fresh from the garden and cooked in a matter of seconds. These hold the greatest magic.

Next come the big and pungent country dishes, the fish stews and soups, the curries and pilaffs, the smoky bean pots, the *pâté Lorraine,* the *fabada,* the *cassoulet.* The savoury messes of vegetables, artichokes and *aubergines* and peppers, the *garbure* of the Basque countries, the *aiouli* of Provence, the *bouride.* The *pasticcios* of Italy — large, convivial, drunk-making *plats régionaux* which for that afternoon turn the world into a warmer and better place.

Then, on another scale, there are *les bonnes choses,* the perennial Great Good Things. Caviar, of course; oysters, smoked salmon. *Foie gras.* The incomparable sea urchin. Virginia ham, the hams of Parma. The black truffle, the white truffle, the egg.

———◆———

ANTHONY WEST ⅌ A SEAFOOD MENU   Here is a very pleasant luncheon menu which can be handled by anyone who has learned to use an oyster knife: per person —

1 dozen oysters on the half shell

Slice of Brie cheese

Watercress salad

Whole meal bread

Comice or Scarlet Bartlett pear or a Golden Delicious apple

½ bottle brut champagne

Coffee

3

A MENU WITH STEAK A simple meal which takes exactly ten minutes to prepare: per person —

1 tenderloin steak with lettuce salad

Stilton cheese with English wheatmeal biscuits

Pear or apple

Glass of Beaujolais or Burgundy

Coffee

The salad may be mixed and the table set while the steak, rubbed on both sides with salt and freshly-ground pepper is under the grill. *Liederkranz* cheese is a good alternative to Stilton in this menu, so is Wenslydale, or any cheese of character.

✦ ✳ ❖ ✳ ✦

LAWRENCE DURRELL  **A LITERARY MENU** Anyone who lives in France has a memoryful of wonderful menus and so many favorite dishes that a restaurant bill of fare is a refined form of torture, but I suppose everyone has an ideal meal, and as a literary man I often dream of sitting down to:

Serial Rights Soup

Sweetbreads *d'Editeur en Brochette*

Canards de Presse

Stuffed Publishers Hearts with Agents Gravy

Roasted Rival with Corn

Sweet and Sour Critic

Fan Flan with Raspberries

With these dishes I would drink Must Hock and Château St. Censor.

MAN RAY ℬ A MENU FOR A DADAIST DAY *Le Petit Dejeuner*. Take a wooden panel of an inch or less thickness, 16 to 20 inches in size. Gather the brightly colored wooden blocks left by children on the floors of playrooms and paste or screw them on the panel. ℬ *Déjeuner*. Take the olives and juice from one  large jar of prepared green or black olives and throw them away. In the empty jar place several steel ball bear ings. Fill the jar with machine oil to prevent rusting. With this delicacy serve a loaf of French bread, 30 inches in length, painted a pale blue. ℬ *Dîner*. Gather wooden darning eggs, one per person. If the variety *without* handles cannot be found, remove the handles. Pierce lengthwise so that skewers can be inserted in each darning egg. Lay the skewered eggs in an oblong or oval pan and cover with transparent cellophane.

MONIKA MANN ℬ IN PRAISE OF SIMPLICITY Somewhere within me, spirit and intellect coincide. That point is the seat of aesthetics, taste, by which we judge the art of cooking and art itself. And isn't my joy at mealtime the marriage of palate and soul? Pleasures of the splendid oaken table with linen and silver and the red damask armchair, behind which the footman waits with ceremonious mien, no longer exist. Now

I pacify myself with the democratic style of plastic table and self-service and stare at the television set, happy not to have to make conversation to my left and to my right and not to have to worry about making a *faux pas!*

Complicated things wear out, simple things don't. That's why I prize vegetables, fresh from the garden of Zachaeus the farmer. His place is about an hour's walk from my house, and, if it isn't raining cats and dogs, I wend my way there. Zachaeus, a barefoot old man, fills my string bag, crosses himself as I leave and murmurs, "enjoy it in peace."

There are little beans, young peas, *finocchi,* tomatoes, spinach and carrots, which I simmer, then garland with radishes and crown with the heart of an artichoke — the so-called Caesar's nut. Olive oil, lemon juice and a little herb salt do the rest. Doesn't God dwell in this platter? Won't it be not only consumed, but painted, celebrated in song? (Oh, ascetics are often saints, but never aesthetes!) A piece of Roquefort cheese and a swallow of Chianti complete the meal. Now I am ready for any feat: an hour with Dostoevsky, a hike round the island, a great rummaging through my studio, a conversation with a little blind dog that often stops by here, and, if I am lucky, a poem.

In the evening there is hot milk with cognac and preserved fruit and whole-grain bread that has been baked only three days ago. In the morning a blood orange, some brown sugar beaten into egg yolk and a little cup of mocha chase my sleep into the wind and make me feel from the ground up what a real blessing eating is!

As for others, I have found honest, even reverential epicures, especially among my painter friends; and gluttons and orgiastic gorgers among the juice-and-strength lads — worthless imitators of Walt Whitman who, for his part, succeeded in bringing the God, not the animal, out of the glutton. "...for I bestow upon any man or woman the entrance of all the gifts of the Universe." By those "gifts of the Universe" the poet-giant from Manhattan certainly had not last in mind the fruits of nature.

Translated by Ronald R. Gilliam.

6

TO BEGIN WITH BREAKFAST

7

JOHN KEATS ℘ COLD COMFORT I: A BREAKFAST People, like dogs, should not be fed more than twice a day. Any diet that includes three squares invariably produces a round folk of fat and flatulence, shortwinded and dewlapped. Consider the Germans, for instance — a people who eat at least four times between dawn and sunset. They are distinguished by adipose skulls, beer bellies, and a language consisting of rumbling belches climaxed by the final eructation of the verb. Yet the Teutons have their

uses, for they have contributed the totem of their tribe, the mast-fed hog, for our delection. Ground hog, properly seasoned, becomes sausage and, hence, breakfast.

To breakfast means to break one's fast. It should be regarded as a time of joy; of new beginnings. It should fortify one for the rigors of the day. I have noticed that it is only secretaries and other pallid office drones who make a breakfast of orange juice, toast and coffee. By this act, they tacitly admit the day to come will prove flaccid, but for the creative man or woman who has work to do, strong meat and drink are requisite. Above all, breakfasts should be varied. Nothing defeats the soul more quickly than the matinal appearance of the egg.

Work then, on a full gut. This is life. And at evensong, a time for repose and reward. In a word, dinner. While breakfast should be merry and robust, dinner should be artistic and contemplative; a distillation, as it were, of the day's fruits. Dinner is the occasion for wit, rather than humor; for companionship after the necessary loneliness of creativity. I strongly suggest that one should breakfast like a peasant, and dine like a viscount. Thus one is reminded that hope depends upon effort; that life is meant to be spent. (There are no doubt other important lessons to be inferred from such symbolism, but since I am not a graduate of Kenyon, nor a subscriber to a small magazine, I feel incompetent to discuss them.)

I have arbitrarily decided that fall is the best season of the year, and therefore suggest a breakfast and a dinner appropriate to the frosty dawns and nights of my Canadian island:

Get up at first light, rising boldly and athletically from beneath the quilts, and dress rapidly before the shaking starts. Set the water on for tea — and charge the teapot. Charge it with Gunpowder tea. Select as many links as you wish of a well-seasoned pork sausage; preferably a sausage that has been prepared by a butcher who has never heard of sage. To fry a sausage is ridiculous. You must prepare it. Wherefore, put the links into a Dutch oven, and pour in enough white wine to cover the bottom of the pan. Cover tightly, and set on a low flame. The object here is to cook the sausages without prematurely breaking the skins. You cook them in a steam of wine, turning them frequently to avoid their sticking, with the accompanying disaster of the premature rupture. (But how does the wine penetrate the unbroken skin? How does air come through a brick wall? The same principle is at work here: you convert the wine into a gas, which penetrates the microscopic pores of the skin. In any event, cook them gently in wine.)

No doubt you have lentils. Sausage without lentils is somewhat like hot without dog. Moreover, no doubt you have had the good judgment (ever thinking of the morrow) to have baked the soaked lentils the day before, baking them traditionally with the pork rind and the cloves. There are people who would have you mash them into a subsequent paste, adding cream, but these people run to chintz. Take, then, yesterday's baked lentils, dunking them in the fat of a strip of bacon which, removed from the pan, you thoughtfully crumple into a million fragments. (What with the tea, the sausage and the lentils, we are now using three burners of the stove, but one object, among others, is to get warm. The kitchen is now warming, but we are by no means through.) Slash a French loaf into the usual rough slices, preparing the slices with garlic butter, and shove into the oven. While these goodies are hotting up, you may begin to consider the vegetable. If your house, like an author's, makes use of every scrap, no doubt there are left-

9

over vegetables — in this case, left-over cauliflower. The fourth burner is now devoted to the cauliflower. Some butter in the pan; when this is melted, work in a bit of cider, in celebration of the fact that it is fall, and because cider in the cauliflower is something that cauliflower badly needs. Begin the vegetable; work the bits of bacon into the lentils, flavoring that dish with Worcestershire sauce or, if you have the cast-iron stomach staunch enough for this breakfast, a judicious amount of Tabasco. (Have a thought to the sausages — turn them. Do they need a few more drops of wine? Tea water boiling yet? How's the bread? Keeping busy keeps one warm.) With all going well, begin the chopping of the chives. Snip the new green ends (I presume everyone grows his chives) into infinitesimal fragments and dust these over the cider-smelling cauliflower. Nutmeg? If you wish; I, frankly, do not, but my children do.

Commence the steeping of the tea. From the liquor closet, obtain the bottle of 150-proof Jamaica Navy rum. By this time, all is ready; load the heated plates — which no doubt you have put into the oven at the last, above the rack that holds the loaf — and prepare to break the fast. Lace the strong tea with the rum. I have had guests call this meal a dog's breakfast, and I agree with them. It is. It is specifically designed for people who work like dogs and who, during the day, therefore lead much the life. But it also has the virtues of thrift and strong flavors and it sustains mind and body until the westering sun falls into the arms of the distant, dark white pines.

Tea, preferably Gunpowder

Pork sausage links

White wine

Baked lentils

Loaf of French bread

Garlic, butter

Cauliflower

Cider

10

Worcestershire sauce or Tabasco

Chives

150-proof Jamaica Navy rum

IRA WALLACH  GINTALOUPE This is my favorite breakfast dish, concocted in Bucks County after a night of depressing normalcy.

Gin

Cantaloupe

Maraschino cherry

Halve the cantaloupe. Scoop out the seeds. Fill the hollow with gin. Drop in the cherry. Allow to steep for two minutes. Eat.

JEAN AMES  SWEET PATOUTI OF PADUA HILLS Cut everything up, adding honey (or sugar, and/or hooch). Keep cutting everything up until it is soft. At the end, add the sliced banana. Serve for breakfast.

1 med. size grapefruit

¼ tsp. cinnamon

⅓ cup seedless raisins

1 banana

11

Panicle of Oat (*Avena sativa*).

MAX EASTMAN  OATMEAL To understand this dish you have to get back to the mood of the old farm or the rural parsonage where maybe you had the good luck to be born. You have to forget all about such fine points of genteel culture as twisting the lemon-peel counter-clockwise in making a martini. That too, of course, is important, but oatmeal is not like that. Oatmeal belongs with the earth and sky, the eternal values. It used to be called "Scotch Oatmeal," and then "Irish Oatmeal," and now, just to fool the kids, "Mother's Oats." In Russia it is, or was, called "Hercules." In England you'll get something like it if you ask for "porridge," although porridge doesn't really mean anything but purée, and purée is decidedly and absolutely not oatmeal.

Oatmeal is thick and sticky. If you pile it up, it will stay piled. It will never subside. It will never sink down into a purée or a pool, no matter what you do to it.

On the old farm it used to be cooked all night, but that was before oats got rolled or "quaked," or whatever they did to change them from horse food into human. Don't let your conservative instincts deceive you into thinking that this old-fashioned procedure is still necessary. It doesn't make the slightest difference. More than most arts, the art of making oatmeal consists in having a clear conception of the goal. You take a certain amount of water — it doesn't matter how much, for you can add more or boil the mixture longer. Add a cup or more of oatmeal and a pinch of salt. The size of a "pinch" has never been accurately determined, and can not be reasoned out. It must be left to the Unconscious. After that there remains no problem except to keep on boiling, and stir with energy and enthusiasm after you reach the point of the pool or purée. The

12

end product must be firmly mountainous, but mealy and malleable.

In serving, you must add plenty of thick cream and a snowfall of sugar. If in your childhood you were not allowed to have sugar on your oatmeal, you will probably use more now than is lastingly desirable. So beware of that historic accident.

And one final caution: Don't keep on eating oatmeal through motives of economy after you have had enough. Whatever is left can be stowed in the refrigerator and used —once more with plenty of cream and sugar—as next day's dessert. For oatmeal like beefsteak is not only just as good, but better cold than hot.

SAMUEL BURI ♫ ROSTI—SWISS PEASANTS' BREAKFAST Peel and boil potatoes. Fry bacon, cut into pieces, in a frying pan. Brown sliced onions; slice the potatoes and in the same pan, cook very slowly until they are golden brown. Salt if necessary. The Swiss mountain peasants eat this with black bread and Emmental cheese. Serves 4.

2 potatoes

4 strips bacon

2 medium onions

Black bread

Emmental cheese

LENN KANENSON ♫ FRIDAY MORNING PANCAKE OMELET AFTER THURSDAY'S CORNED BEEF AND CABBAGE Blend pancake flour and baking powder with a fork. Add milk and mix. Follow with drippings and yellow of one egg. The egg white is beaten with a fork using arm muscle until the white is foamy—no gadgets. Fold into mixture. Now break the other 3 eggs into the mixture but throw away the shells.

Toss the butter into an iron skillet with a medium heat and melt. How one uses the corned beef is a question of cooking skill. If you are chicken, make one omelet-size pancake and lay in the corned beef after pouring the batter. If you are a fencing master, lay in the corned beef strips and then pour the batter. The pancake omelet should look golden brown with bright yellow streaks through it. Check the cooking side by lifting an edge. Flip the omelet flippantly when it is brown, set, and bubbles popping. When ready, add syrup, jelly, or any other maniacal twist you are prone to, and eat.

Naturally, I've thought of substitutes for the corned beef. Anyway, if you don't make the omelet correctly the first time, persevere or you can always stab yourself with the fork.

Leftover cold corned beef (sliced thin)

1 cup pancake flour (your favorite colored box)

1 cup milk

$\frac{1}{3}$ teaspoon baking powder

4 eggs

2 tablespoons bacon drippings (in liquid state)

$\frac{1}{4}$ pound butter

✄ CONRAD AIKEN ✄

THE ONLY RECIPE BY AIKEN —

ONE NOT DERIVED FROM SHAKESPEARE-BACON —

IS: ANY REALLY SENSIBLE CHAP'LL

FRY AN APPLE WITH HIS SCRAPPLE.

14

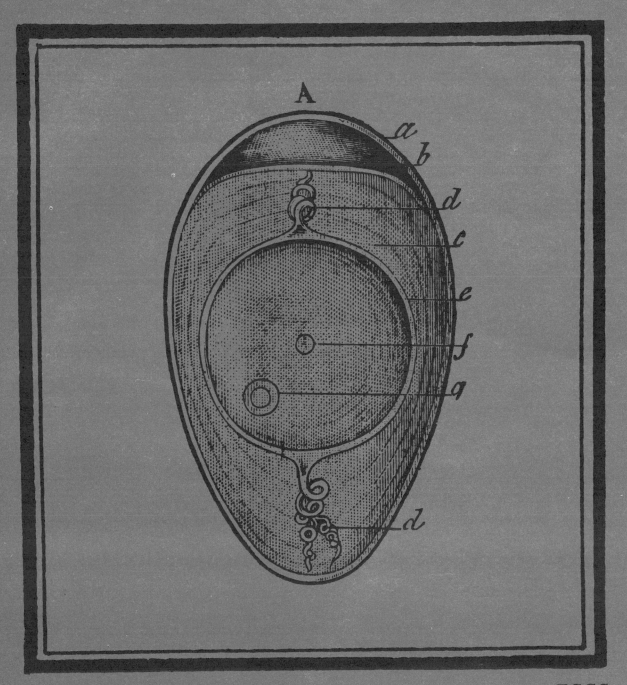

A

a
b
d
c
e
f
g
d

EGGS

15

ALLAN SEAGER ⚜ SEAGER'S SCRAMBLED EGGS I believe everything today should be made as difficult as possible so as to combat creeping informality, "His 'n Hers" steaks, TV dinners *et al.* ⚜ This homely dish begins with a buttered baking dish in which is strewn a layer of chopped sautéed mushrooms, a layer of grated Parmesan cheese, a layer of bechamel sauce, the scrambled eggs, a thick layer of bechamel sauce, a thick layer of Parmesan cheese, which, after being browned under a *salamandre* (ha ha!) or a broiler is covered with a quarter pound of melted butter and served. ⚜ THE MUSHROOMS About a cupful, chopped fine, turned in butter over a low fire for a few minutes. A couple of tablespoons of dry sherry, or, if a sweeter taste is preferred, of bual Madeira may be added. ⚜ THE BECHAMEL SAUCE To a cup and a half of chicken broth placed in a shallow pan over medium heat, add three or four slices of carrot, three or four slices of onion, a piece of bay leaf about the size of half a matchbox and eight or ten peppercorns. Reduce to three-quarters cup. Strain and reserve. ⚜ To two ounces of butter melted in a saucepan, add two tablespoons of flour. Stir until mixed into a paste. Start adding over low heat the reserved chicken broth and keep stirring. As it thickens, add scalded thin cream, stirring until sauce is the desired thickness. Bring to boil for one minute. Reserve. ⚜ THE EGGS Allow two eggs for each eater. Take a cup of whipping cream and whip until you can turn the dish upside down without the cream falling out. Break the eggs one at a time into the cream and whip slowly until they are mingled. ⚜ Beforehand, have a well-buttered double boiler on the stove. Pour in the mixture of cream and eggs and start scraping them off the sides and bottom which is the only sane way to scramble eggs because you can control abso-

16

lutely the degree of moisture. Since these eggs are to go under a broiler, they should be finished rather more moist than you would care to eat them. § Put the dish together as instructed in the first paragraph. Place under the *salamandre* (ha ha!) or broiler until the cheese is brown and tending to bubble. Pour over it the previously melted quarter pound of butter and eat. § These will be the best scrambled eggs you have ever eaten.

ROBERT OSBORN § OMELETTE FINES HERBES The trick is to have a *thick* frying pan which is HOT. The nut of butter dropped in should sizzle but not jump. Break two eggs into a glass. Add salt, pepper, *fines herbes* (chive, CHERVIL, a pinch of tarragon, parsley — all chopped fine). With a spoon beat the eggs until they are broken up but not whipped. Heat a plate to receive the omelette. Test the pan with butter. If the temperature is correct, pour in the eggs. Roll pan as soon as a thin, cooked layer has developed. Fold half the layer back and roll more uncooked egg into the exposed portion of the pan. Roll back the other half of the layer and complete the fill-in. Roll it all out onto the warm plate. A slowly-cooked omelette is a poorly-cooked omelette.

RALPH JOHNSON § BRICKLAYER'S OMELET Fry three strips of fat bacon in a nine-inch iron skillet until not too crisp.

Crack four eggs in a bowl

Add: ½ cup flour

1 cup milk

A little less than one teaspoon baking powder

Salt and freshly-ground black pepper

⅓ cup chopped olives

⅓ cup chopped bell pepper

⅓ cup diced Monterey jack cheese

Stir above thoroughly. Remove bacon from skillet and leave grease. Pour mixed ingredients into skillet, crumble bacon on top. Put into oven about 350 degrees. Bake until the omelet stands above the edge of the skillet about two or three inches. Be sure to watch it as it comes from the oven as it is marvelous to behold — it deflates very quickly. This serves two. A little jelly is sometimes good with it.

Something else quite tasty: Add a large spoonful of cottage cheese with chives to two eggs and scramble.

CLANCY SIGAL ⌂ PIZZA WITHOUT THE PIE In a very large frying pan on a medium flame, place some large dabs of butter. When the butter is sizzling, sprinkle in some salt and pepper. Then slice fresh tomatoes and cover the bottom of the pan with a single layer. Cover the pan and let the tomatoes cook for five minutes. For every two servings pour in from four to six well-beaten eggs. Add salt and pepper. Cover and let the eggs solidify, being very careful that they do not burn on the bottom. Before the eggs are ready to eat, place slices of provolone cheese on top, let it melt and then on top of it sprinkle not-too-much oregano. (Thyme will do in a pinch, but oregano is preferable.) Cover. When Jesus nods, remove the lid and use a spatula to chisel the eggs and tomatoes away from the bottom.

Butter, large dabs

Salt and pepper

Fresh, sliced tomatoes

Four to six eggs for every two servings

Provolone cheese, sliced

Oregano (or thyme in a pinch)

RALPH STACKPOLE ♫ PACHADE AUVERGNATE Grate one good-sized potato and chop one onion very fine. Beat two eggs slightly and season with salt and pepper. Add the grated potato and chopped onion. Fry in butter, flipping over like a pancake to cook the other side. The mixture to be fried at one time should not be over 1 centimetre thick in the pan. Each *pachade* is a single serving.

ROGER BARR ♫ HUEVOS RANCHEROS Place the ingredients in the earthenware dishes. On each broken egg place a dab of sweet cream to keep the yolks soft. Sprinkle with salt and freshly-ground pepper and bake in a medium (350 degrees) oven for about 12 minutes, or until the whites of the eggs have cooked. The *chorizo* will flavor the whole dish. For *each* serving, you need:

An earthenware dish, flat and round

Two eggs, fresh

Two tablespoons of precooked peas

Two slices of tomato

A small slice of ham

Two or three slices of *chorizo,* (or pepperoni)

Salt and freshly-ground black pepper

A dab of fresh cream

MICHEL LARIONOV  BAKED EGGS IN TOMATO CUPS Cut large tomatoes in half (two tomatoes for four servings), remove the pulp and drain. Into each tomato half, break an egg, dot with butter and sprinkle with salt and freshly-ground pepper. Bake in a moderate oven until the eggs are firm. These may be served covered with a hot cream sauce seasoned with curry powder.

Cream Sauce (for four servings): Melt four tablespoons of butter in a heavy saucepan over low heat. Add two tablespoons of flour and blend. Then add two cups of rich milk or cream, slowly, stirring constantly. Add ¼ teaspoon of salt, a dash of white pepper and one teaspoon of curry powder. Cover and cook for 5 to 8 minutes.

TO BEGIN AGAIN: APPETIZERS

21

Herring (*Clupea harengus*).
(From Report of U. S. Fish Commission, 1884.)

STANLEY WILLIAM HAYTER 🐟 HOT HERRING Fillet the herring with your thumbnail, a razor blade or small knife and cut into large bite-size pieces. Place into a bowl containing the juice of four lemons. Add salt, chopped celery leaf and chopped fresh red pepper or cayenne powder as desired. Let stand for several hours. Serve as hors d'oeuvres or anytime for the promotion of drinking. This amount should serve a party of 8 to 12 adequately.

This recipe is to be used only when the herring is so fresh that it looks at you with a bright red eye. The result is hot as hell, sweet, fresh and raw.

2 pounds of fresh, raw herring

Juice of four lemons

Chopped celery leaf

Chopped fresh red pepper (or cayenne powder)

Dash of salt

RICHARD EMIL BRAUN 🐟 TO LAY ON TOAST OR SALADS Chop a quantity of kippered herring and one-third that amount of pimiento-stuffed olives. Mingle, adding vinegar from the olive bottle, some oil, a generous scoop of chopped oregano, and a couple of finely-flitched scallions. Shoot a half-dozen hard dashes of Tabasco on top. Dust with garlic powder.

Cover with sunflower-seed kernels to one-fifth the height of the whole. Mix well again, introducing a few capers to surprise. Let this repose a half hour before using.

(Roman antiquity ate a similar mélange, which, because of the abundance of dry wine, did no harm detectable today by the methods of modern historical research.)

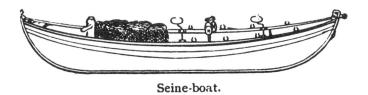

Seine-boat.

Kippered herring
Pimiento-stuffed olives and their vinegar
Oil
Chopped oregano
Scallions
Tabasco
Garlic powder
Sunflower-seed kernels
Capers
With ¼ lb. kippers, adds up to appetizer for 6

EMILE COMPARD ⌘ SARDINES FRAICHES Place the desired number of sardines in a flat pan. Cover them with coarse salt, and leave them overnight. After 12 hours, wash and clean the fish. You will have filets of great delicacy.

The fresh, raw sardines may be eaten with bread and butter and, if you wish, a bit of lemon juice.

GWEN STONE 🔊 L'ANCHOUIADE This recipe has been a mainstay with our family for over twenty years. It comes from an ancient Provencal cookbook. It is the delicious *l'Anchouiade*. It is done with loaves and fishes, and your dinner guests are the spectators of this miraculous feast *al fresco*.

It is begun with anchovies which are boned, soaked in water to remove the salt and arrayed on a platter with olive oil, a pinch of pepper and garlic cut into fine little dice. On another platter are sandwich-sized strips of crust of bread, called *tartines,* an inch and a half thick. On still a third are cubes of bread, preferably of crust consistency, so that they do not crumble easily.

Each guest soaks his cube in the oil over the anchovies and uses it to crush an anchovy on his *tartine*. He munches on the remains of the sauce-soaked cube as he watches his *tartine* toast over an open fire. The ancient cookbook warns, facetiously, "Care must be taken to put out the fire in time as the strong Mediterranean winds will carry the fine garlic perfume to the far ends of Provence." And it has been with the help of our Sausalito squalls that our friends in Belvedere knew we were dining on *l'Anchouiade* and dying to join us.

Anchovies

Olive oil

Pepper

Fresh garlic

Crusts of bread

Cubes of bread of crust consistency

MICHEL MISHORIT 🔊 BASIC SESAME TAHINA RECIPE In a deep bowl mix well the Sesame Tahina with the water until thoroughly mixed. Add the lemon juice, salt and garlic and keep mixing it constantly. Add the Tabasco and let it stand for ten minutes. Sprinkle on top with **paprika and chopped** parsley.

This should be eaten together with a flat bread called Pittah, and dipped with your fingers into the Tahina. It could also be used as a dressing in preparing fish, vegetables or meat dishes. Serves 8 with Pittah dunk.

5 tablespoons of Sesame Tahina* (Sesame Tahina may be bought in a Syrian or Middle Eastern store.)

1 glass of water

1 lemon

½ teaspoon salt

1 teaspoon of paprika

1 clove garlic, minced

1 drop of Tabasco

Chopped parsley

Sesame (*Sesamum Indicum*).

Sesame (*Sesamum Indicum*).

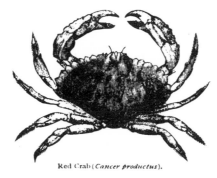

Red Crab (*Cancer productus*).

ELISE CAVANNA 卐 CRAB CAKE Chop crab meat and combine with lemon juice, parsley and ricotta. Mix thoroughly with unbeaten egg whites. Pour into a loaf pan approximately 8 by 5 inches and bake at 350 degrees for 40 minutes. Remove from the

Sesame Tahina is a vegetal oil of peanut butter consistency made from husked sesame seeds.

25

oven and cool in the pan. Place in refrigerator to chill.

Cut into mouthful-size squares, for easy handling. Garnish with thin slices of sweet red pepper when in season. Serves 8.

6 ounces of crab meat

4 heaping tablespoons of ricotta cheese

3 teaspoons of chopped parsley

1 teaspoon of lemon juice

3 egg whites

FELIX RUVULO ⟡ STUFFED MUSHROOMS Remove the stalks from a number of fresh mushrooms. Mix French bread crumbs and grated Romano cheese in a 3 to 1 mixture — a third of cheese. Add finely-chopped fresh garlic and parsley.

Either fill the mushroom caps with the mixture and pour oil over them, or mix a little olive oil with the breadcrumb mixture to moisten it, and then fill the caps.

Broil and serve as hors d'oeuvres.

Fresh mushrooms

French bread crumbs

Grated Romano cheese

Garlic

Parsley

Olive Oil

Editors' note: It is advisable to prepare at least 6 of these mushrooms per person.

YEKTAI  **BORANI** Spinach hors d'oeuvres Boil the desired amount of spinach and let it cool. Chop it and season with salt, pepper, sliced boiled onion and spices to taste. Mix with yoghurt and put in the refrigerator to chill. Serve on a platter and surround with olives, small raw onions and radishes. Serves 6 as hors d'oeuvres.

1 package frozen spinach, or 1 lb. fresh

Salt and pepper

1 large boiled onion

½ cup yoghurt

VELTA SNICKERE  **CEYLONESE AMBROSIA**

The pulp

Of a peeled avocado pear,

(With sugar added)

Is mashed

With a fork.

27

IRA WALLACH 🔊 BOEUF ETIENNE I refer you to a recipe which is from the chapter entitled "Hors d'Oeuvres de Combat" in *Hopalong-Freud*.

1 horse

2 cups sweet cream

Concombres, ciseaux, punaises

(Cucumbers, scissors, tacks)

1 pint any Napoleon '97

Simply curry the horse, and separate the mane from the yolk. Fold, *do not mix,* in double boiler. Drink the Napoleon '97. Place curried horse gently in a bed of *concombres, ciseaux, et punaises,* and bake in a medium oven. Baste every half hour with a dash of *wienerspritzer.* Get another pint of any Napoleon '97.

I have never tasted Boeuf Etienne (we were unable to obtain the Napoleon '97).

COLD SOUPS

29

NOEL BARBER 🦐 ICED SODA WATER SOUP Dishes depending on the addition at the exact moment of three-fifths of a gram or some strange concoction are beyond my powers — not only because my knowledge of arithmetic is small, but because my recipes have often been picked up in remote regions where the inhabitants and I had no common language.

This is what happened with *Iced Soda Water Soup,* which I tasted first in a village in Persia, the morning after an earthquake in which several thousand people were killed in a vast area between Teheran and the Caspian Sea. Since my knowledge of Persian is considerably less than my knowledge of arithmetic, the only thing I could do (after tasting the soup and finding it delightful) was to watch the villagers make it for me all over again and write down just what I saw.

I had raced there to beat my competitors. I flew from London to Teheran, drove eleven hours until I could get no further because of landslides, slept in the car, then did another five hours on horseback.

It was hot, dusty and terrible. I breakfasted off some chocolate and processed cheese and reached the village — which was in the center, the heart, of the devastated area — at noon. Hardly a house was left undamaged, but in one of the few skeletons that stood, pointing up like a rotten old tooth, friendly peasants made me lunch — starting with this soup. It is an ideal soup for a hot day — it should be eaten cold, and because it is a peasant dish, you may vary the ingredients to suit yourself.

3 jars (1¼ pints) of yoghurt

¼ pint of cream

1 heaping tablespoon of raisins

1 heaping tablespoon of dill or, if unobtainable, parsley

1 heaping tablespoon of chopped onion

1½ medium cucumbers

30

3 hard-boiled eggs

Soda water as desired

Chop all the dry ingredients very fine and place in a bowl. Mix with the yoghurt and the cream and add as much soda water as you like just before serving. For 6.

———————•—•———————

VAN WYCK BROOKS 𝔖 ANDALUSIAN GASPACHO To serve six, peel and dice in very small pieces into a large bowl:

Six tomatoes

Two cucumbers

Four pimientos

Reserving the juice

Mince

One large, sweet onion

Mash

Two cloves of garlic

(Or skewer garlic on a toothpick and remove before serving the soup.) Add:

Four tablespoons of vinegar, and

Four tablespoons of olive oil

Salt

Freshly-ground pepper, and

Tabasco to taste

One cup of ice water

Chill in the refrigerator overnight or for at least an hour. The bulk of the soup will increase as it chills. Serve with an ice cube in each soup plate.

MERVIN JULES ♫ CURRY VICHYSOISSE MIMOSA Fry leeks and onion in two tablespoons of butter until golden (not brown). Then add potatoes, chicken broth and salt. Boil these ingredients for forty minutes, then pass the liquid through a sieve. To the strained liquid add the milk, curry and sherry. Bring to a boil (do not boil) and cool. Chill. Serve cold and float on the soup in each cup the yolk of hard-boiled eggs which has been crumbled to resemble mimosa blossoms, and sprigs of parsley to resemble mimosa branches. Serves 8.

4 leeks

1 medium onion, sliced

5 medium potatoes, peeled and sliced

1 quart chicken broth

2 tablespoons butter

1 tablespoon salt

4 cups milk

2 teaspoons curry powder

½ cup sherry

EPHREM WEITZMAN ♫ BORSCHT WITH POTATO Peel and grate 5 large beets and one large onion. Bring to a boil in one and a half quarts of water. Simmer for 45 minutes. Cool. Add the following ingredients to taste: cubed hard cooked eggs, sliced or cubed cucumbers, scallions, juice of half a lemon, two tablespoons or more brown sugar, three or more tablespoons sour cream, salt and dill to taste. Add, while still hot, a cup or more boiled new potatoes. The last addition is important, and it is important that the potatoes be hot. Borscht should be sweet and is always served chilled. Serves 8.

5 large beets

1 large onion

2 hard-cooked eggs

2 cucumbers

3 scallions

Juice of half a lemon

Two tablespoons brown sugar

Three or more tablespoons sour cream

Salt

Dill

6 boiled small new potatoes

NATHALIE GONCHAROVA ♫ BORSCHT ODESSA Grate 2 or more ounces of ripe beets which have been cooked until tender, and press through a sieve. Add the water in which they were cooked and enough kvass* to make four cups of liquid. Add herbs as desired: 1 teaspoon chives, dill, etc. Salt and pepper lightly. Chill thoroughly before serving. Serves four.

*Kvass is a light, sour beer made in Russia from rye or barley.

NANCY HALE ✍ DANVILLE DE LUXE CONSOMME This is a form of jellied soup which I was served at a ladies' lunch in Danville, Virginia, before a lecture I gave there, and, I think, in its flavor — one of those magic and inevitable blends, as *right* as turkey and cranberry — it sums up the Lucullan qualities of Southern ladies enjoying "havin' everythin' nice."

The lunch was given by an elderly Southern lady in an overwhelmingly comfortable house (the House of Usher was only one type of Southern mansion, the uncomfortable type) with an elderly colored butler serving, and terrific Spode for service plates. We had previously been served, by the butler, "old-fashioneds," which still thrive in houses where trouble is no object, together with little hot cheese biscuits.

I must say that, although I am a Yankee and a Bostonian and a Unitarian and a Liberal, I wallow in pleasure when it is served out like that with a large silver ladle. There is so little left of it nowadays, not, heaven knows, because there isn't the money for it, but because so many people have lost track of what comfort feels like.

Anyway, after our cocktails we strolled into the dining room — brilliantly sunny through swags of white brocade, and were served, first, what I think I will call:

DANVILLE DE LUXE CONSOMME

Put some cans of Consommé Madrilene in the icebox to stiffen. When you open them to serve, break up the jellied soup into fragments — it looks prettier so. Put into luncheon soup cups, top with two tablespoons sour cream, and top *that* with a heaping tablespoon of red caviar.

34

HOT SOUPS

JEAN VARDA 🦁 BEAUTIFUL SOUP As Jean Varda tells it, some young students of his opened a hamburger stand and asked him to paint them a sign. At the very bottom of a long list of London-burgers, Madrid-burgers, Paris-burgers, Vienna-burgers, Rome-burgers, New York-burgers appeared the Ostrogotz-Plakatz-burger. The young students prospered for it seemed that no one could walk past that stand without asking for an Ostrogotz-Plakatz-burger (which is, incidentally the name of a small Polish town which Varda happened to pick out of the newspaper). What's in a name? good eating — voila!

Embolon.— Ulysses and the Sirens

The Beautiful Soup (Avgolemono)

1 quart stock (chicken or beef)

1 cup cut-up chicken or other pieces of meat

1 cup rice

4 lemons

4 eggs

Heat stock, add meat or chicken. Cook rice in stock until soft (10 or 15 min.) When rice is cooked beat eggs and slowly add lemon juice, beating constantly to keep eggs from curdling. Add egg and lemon mixture to boiling soup, stirring until cooked. Serves 4.

This is a classic soup recipe of many countries, but the lemon is characteristic of hot southern European climates where lots of oil is used in the cooking. Where olive trees are growing, lemon trees grow by their side.

36

EMLEN ETTING 🔊 CHICKEN FOG SOUP Take a glass of bouillon per person and heat slowly. Break a raw egg (one per portion) and beat it up in a bowl. When the soup begins to simmer, pour in the egg and allow it to remain for 30 seconds on the stove, stirring rapidly before serving. On cold days, a jigger of tequila thrown in is a comfort.

Chicken bouillon

Raw egg, beaten

Variation: jigger of tequila

Editor's note: For another variation try wine instead of tequila. Add cold wine to beaten egg and sweeten with sugar. For a fancier fog, add wine to yolks and beat, then fold in whites. Another variation: add lemon and/or milk.

VERNON WATKINS 🔊 LEEK BROTH (CAWL CENNIN) Melt a tablespoon of drippings in a heavy saucepan. Slice the leeks and fry them gently in the drippings for a few minutes. Add a dessertspoonful* of plain flour. Gradually add the stock.

Leek (*Allium tricoccum.*)
1, flowering plant; 2, the plant with the leaves developed; *a*, flower; *b*, fruit; *c*, seed.

The dessertspoon used by the Welsh and Irish is approximately the size of our soupspoon or tablespoon.

Bring to a boil. Add lentils. Season to taste. Leave to simmer for at least two hours. The longer, the better; up to two days. Chop parsley into saucepan before serving. Serves 4.

1 quart of stock made from a veal bone

2 leeks

Lentils to taste, about 2 tablespoonfuls

Flour

MATSUMI KANEMITSU  GREEN NOODLE SOUP In a covered saucepot put

4 cups of beef broth

Dice and add 1 onion

Slice and add 1½ tomatoes

Finish with 1 ounce of green noodles

Cook ten minutes

Then serve 4.

LAWRENCE DURRELL  POTAGE DE POIS CHICHES When I first lived in France I discovered through sheer penury what has become a firm favorite of mine since I no longer have to eat it every day. It could be called *Wolf at Bay Soup* or *The Peasant's Gift to the Poor Poet*. The prosaic local cooks simply call it *Potage de Pois Chiches*.

Soak chickpeas overnight, drain and put through a coarse mincer, keeping a handful apart to add later. In a thick, deep pot (or even a pressure cooker, but this kills the garlic) put stock (or even water, at the end of the month), the minced chickpeas, thyme, bay leaf, celery, and a whole head of peeled but not chopped garlic; pepper and salt (be generous with the pepper and the salt, too, if you cannot afford to add bacon). Cook for an hour, well-covered. Then add wine, remaining chickpeas, and cook for a further hour or until it is thick, over a low flame, stirring occasionally to prevent sticking. Remove the herbs and the bacon, and serve very hot with crisp French bread, a good green salad and a piece of cheese to follow. This makes a very substantial meal for four hungry people (or one hungry writer four days running). It is even better when re-heated and costs about 7 cents per head.

Chick-pea (*Cicer arietinum*).

½ pound chickpeas
2 pints stock or water
Thyme, bay leaf, celery
Garlic, whole head, peeled but not chopped
Pepper, salt
Piece of fat bacon
Glass of red wine

MERVIN JULES 𝕊 **POYSTER SOUP**   Soak overnight in one and a half cups of water, 2 cups of whole, dried green peas. The following day, drain off the water and rinse the peas several times. Place the peas in a soup kettle with the following:

6 cups of fresh water

2 onions

½ pound of salt pork

8 whole peppercorns, slightly bruised

1 generous teaspoon of salt

1 large ham bone, with scraps of meat clinging to it

(don't forget the peas)

Bring these ingredients to a boil, then simmer for three hours. Remove the pork and ham bone and pour the other contents through a sieve, mashing the peas and onions through as well. Add:

1 cup of fresh ground or chopped oysters

Bring the soup to a boil and serve with diced salt pork and chopped, fresh parsley. Serves 6.

Shell of an Oyster (*Ostræa virginica*)

ANTHONY WEST 𝕊 **BEAN SOUP**   *Country Mutton Stew*   makes the centre of a good meal. Another excellent kind of country meal consists simply of a good soup, bread and cheese, and a glass of wine. The soup to play its part here must be a not-too-distant cousin of a stew. Here is a good robust *Bean Soup:*

40

Take a pound of white haricot beans or navy beans. Set them to soak overnight, and three hours before the soup is wanted start them simmering gently in just enough water to cover. Then take a good-sized white cabbage and cut it into strips, peel and quarter six medium-sized potatoes, slice a couple of big carrots, skin and quarter the turnip, roll up rashers of fat bacon and tie them with string, add bouquet of herbs, cloves of garlic and peppercorns, and put them all with ham bone into a second pan, filled with boiling, slightly salted water. This second pan should be started so that it is ready at the end of the three hours, when the beans will have just taken up all the water in their pot. The beans should then be put in with the vegetables and the ham bone taken out. When the vegetables and beans have been stirred together the soup is ready to eat. Serves 6.

1 pound of white haricot or navy beans

1 white cabbage

6 medium-sized potatoes

Couple of big carrots

1 turnip

Four rashers of fat bacon

Bouquet of herbs

Two cloves of garlic

Peppercorns

Large ham bone

KURT SONDERBORG ⌥ SAURESUPPE Place a smoked ham bone with some meat on it into a large kettle of boiling water. Add sliced fresh carrots, peas, asparagus tips and chives. Then add dried fruit as desired, prunes, apples, pears, apricots, etc. Add oregano, celery leaf, bay leaf, marjoram, thyme and salt. Then make the soup a little more sour with lemon juice, and counter that flavor with sugar. It should have a strong sweet-sour taste. The soup may be thickened with a sauce of melted butter and flour. Cook on a low fire.

Now prepare a noodle or dumpling dough with 2 beaten eggs, ½ teaspoon of salt, 2 tablespoons of hot water and a cup of flour, adding the flour to the other ingredients until the dough is stiff. Drop the dumplings from a spoon into the simmering soup. When the dumplings rise to the surface, they are cooked.

In Germany this soup is often served with boiled eel. It is a success if in cold weather it makes the sweat pour from your face. Serves 8.

Ham bone

4 carrots, sliced, raw

1 cup peas, raw

6 asparagus tips

¼ cup chives, cut small

½ lb. dried fruit (prunes, apples, pears, apricots, etc.)

Pinch of oregano

Celery leaf

Bay leaf

Pinch of marjoram

Pinch of thyme, or 2 fresh leaves

Salt to taste

Lemon juice to taste

Sugar to taste

A thickening sauce of butter and flour

Dumpling dough:

2 beaten eggs

½ teaspoon of salt

2 tablespoons of hot water

1 cup of flour

BERTON ROUECHE ❧ MORE THAN MINESTRONE The food faddist is a pa-
thetic creature. He is credulous (for the belief that certain foods have panacean qualities has no basis in scientific fact), his attitude toward food is narcissistic (for he eats to
move his bowels, trim his waistline, give lustre to his hair), and the food that he is currently obliged to eat (wheat germ, yoghurt, gelatin, honey and vinegar, carrot juice) is
revolting. But more than that, his approach to food is crass, philistine, barbaric. He is
insensitive to the art of cookery. He takes his food as he finds it in its package — raw,
ready-made, miscellaneous. And cooking, though perhaps a humble and homely art, is
nevertheless an art. For the cook's achievement, like that of any artist, is to create something that is greater than the sum of its parts.

Soak overnight:

1½ cups red kidney beans

½ cup blackeye peas

Drain them. Add them to:

3 quarts stock (ham bone, or the water in which a ham

or smoked tenderloin butt has been cooked)

Simmer the beans and peas until they are tender. Chop until fine:

½ cup sliced onions

½ cup carrots

1 clove garlic

4 tablespoons parsley

Heat in a saucepan:

½ cup oil

Sautè the vegetables in the oil until they are golden brown. Add:

1 can tomato paste

1 cup coarsely shredded cabbage

1 cup chickpeas

2 tablespoons brown sugar

2 teaspoons basil

¼ teaspoon salt

¼ teaspoon pepper

Simmer these ingredients for 5 minutes. Add them to the cooked beans and blackeye peas. Add:

1 cup boiled elbow macaroni

Simmer the soup 1 hour longer. Serve with grated Parmesan cheese. Enough for 12-15.

The Upper Part of *Ocimum Basilicum*, with flowers.

KATHERINE ANNE PORTER ♫ FRESH VEGETABLE BORSCHT I love
Kosher cooking, and when I was in Germany years ago I haunted a fine Kosher restaurant where they practiced discrimination against us goyim by putting us on one side
of the restaurant and serving us out of unsanctified crockery, while the true Kosher
God-chosen ate in peace and purity on the other side. But they did give us the same
delicious food, and I developed a passion for chopped liver, gefilte fish, pancakes with
cottage cheese and sour cream, but above all, BORSCHT.

This is an original *receipt,* as they used to call them in the South. I do not want to
add false hopes, but this vegetable broth is the most delightful drink when you are hungry and yet do not want to eat because you are trying to lose weight. (I do not have
this problem; I have weighed in at point 115 for the past five years, but I love this broth
and drink it nearly every day.) It nourishes and satisfies you, and helps you to hang on
until the next meal. You can make it by the gallon and put it in containers—1 quart
perhaps is the best—in the deep freeze where it may freeze up and be useful for months.

Ingredients for a gallon:
20 large beets
1 medium-size white cabbage
8 or 10 large stalks of celery with leaves
2 very large onions
1 bunch large carrots
½ pound fresh grapes (crush a little)

2 sweet apples (sweet and tart)

About 20 whole black peppercorns

Don't peel anything except the onions. Strip celery stalks and break in pieces. Trim the carrots and beets slightly, top and bottom. Chop onions and cabbage and carrots and beets and apples small enough to pack well, after scrubbing everything in floods of warm water; be sure not to leave one grain of sand or grit. Pack into kettle that has a tight lid. Add:

2 tablespoons monosodium glutamate or Accent

2 tablespoons salt

Cover with water to the top of the kettle. I use for this amount of vegetable, a kettle that holds just 1 gallon, 3 and ¾ quarts liquid without the vegetables. Let the vegetables simmer slowly until done but not overcooked; the point of this broth is the fresh flavor. Strain off the broth through a large sieve, or colander, then once more through a cloth. I just use a large cup towel, newly rinsed in cold water to remove the faint flavor of laundry soap. Add then more salt or monosodium if you like, but no pepper. The peppercorns, strained off and discarded with the rest will have left their aroma. This can be drunk hot or cold, with a dollop of sour cream if you wish. I drink it cold without cream.

⟶ ✳ ❧❦❧ ✳ ⟵

Note: In season, instead of grapes, for this amount of vegetables, you may leave out the grapes and add a well-washed, pressed-down quart of fresh sorrel, which gives a delicious tang if you care for sorrel.

This broth came out of my attempts to master the secret of Kosher borscht, which I never did, but arrived at this instead.

46

ROBERT HILLYER 🔊 SOUP GLORIANA The only chance I ever had to become a cook was when I went cruising in my sloop *Gloriana*. Then I discovered some delicious combinations — such as clam bouillon with green pea soup.

Pea-blossom

RICHARD OLNEY 🔊 TWO POT-AU-FEU All my favorite dishes are absolutely classic. Certainly each has its variations, but only the *pot-au-feu* has as many as there are cooks (*bouillabaisse* and *cassoulet* may run some competition). Each cook thinks his best and I have never tasted better than mine (I have never tasted Dodin Bouffant's). For a great *pot-au-feu* one must make two — but, first, the pot is important. It should be earthenware — lacking that, cast iron. If it is new earthenware, season it — that is to say, rub it inside and out with garlic, fill with water and several cloves of garlic and boil for several hours. Nearly everyone now is victim of the gas flame, so the precaution of an asbestos mat is necessary. If you plan to share a *pot-au-feu* with several guests, make one the day before for the family:

POT-AU-FEU No. 1:

Toss in the pot a couple of pounds of ox tail, onions, carrots, turnips (several of each), some bones (veal or beef), a *bouquet garni* containing a large branch of thyme, a bay leaf and some parsley, a small handful of coarse salt (sea salt is best), and fill the pot with cold water. Bring to a boil, skim, and barely simmer until the meat is done. Don't eat the soup that night — but prepare a tomato sauce to accompany the ox tail in order to make it as different as possible from the following day's meal. Strain the bouillon through a sieve and return it to the pot. Serves 8.

NEXT DAY, POT-AU-FEU No. 2:

Add bones and adjust the quantity of yesterday's broth with water. Bring to a boil, and then add, well tied up, about three pounds of the gelatinous meat from a hindleg of beef, and half as much of the fattier meat from the side of the animal; an entire head (not a clove), untouched, of garlic, an apple, a healthy handful of dried *cèpes* (they can be found in any Italian store in American cities — simply called dried mushrooms), and a *bouquet garni* as before, but this time including a small branch of rosemary and either a bunch of chervil or a branch of tarragon — or both. No salt. Add a branch of celery and a few peppercorns. Bring again to a boil, skim, throw in a glass of cold water, boil, skim again, lower the fire to a bare simmer and cook, leaving the lid slightly ajar, for two hours. Now add (if in season — otherwise make shift with winter versions) a bunch of peeled new carrots, a bunch of peeled new turnips, several leeks (the dark green leaves cut off) tied together, two or three onions, one of which is stuck with two cloves, and continue to simmer until the meat is done — probably another two hours. Some people toss in a chicken and change the name to *petite marmite,* but I find that this muddies the flavor. An hour before serving, clean, cut in quarters, and pass a few minutes in boiling water a green cabbage. Drain it and put to cook separately — gently with a ladleful of bouillon (sometimes I eliminate the cabbage and simply toss into the pot — one for each guest — some artichokes). Half an hour later, in another pan, boil some peeled new potatoes, also with bouillon.

Discard the celery, the onion stuck with cloves, the apple and the *bouquet garni.* Skim off excess fat. Place slices of dried, slightly toasted (in the oven) bread (not that depressing imitation of cake which is the packaged variety) in the soup plates, a chunk of Parmesan and a cheese grater on the table, and ladle the bouillon directly from the pot. Soup finished, cut the strings from the meat and the leeks and serve the meat — to be sliced at the table — on the largest available platter. Surround by separate heaps of cabbage (or artichokes), potatoes, carrots, turnips, and leeks, and accompany it with a dish of coarse salt, a dish of sour gherkins, and a pot of French mustard. Serve a single light red wine (in abundance), a bit of salad, cheese, and fruit, and there is a beautiful meal. For 8.

POT-AU-FEU No. 1 — *FOR THE FAMILY*

A couple of pounds of ox-tail

Several onions

Several carrots

Several turnips

Some bones (veal or beef)

A *bouquet garni* — a large branch of thyme,

a bay leaf, and some parsley

A small handful of coarse salt

A tomato sauce for the ox-tail

POT-AU-FEU No. 2 — *FOR GUESTS*

Bones

Three pounds of the gelatinous meat from a hindleg of beef

One and a half pounds of fattier meat from the side of a cow

A *head* of garlic

An apple

A handful of dried *cèpes* (mushrooms)

A *bouquet garni* (as above, but including a branch of rosemary and either a bunch of chervil or a branch of tarragon — or both)

A branch of celery

A few peppercorns

A bunch of peeled new carrots

A bunch of peeled new turnips

Several leeks

Two or three onions (one stuck with cloves)

Cloves

A green cabbage or artichokes (one for each guest)

Some peeled new potatoes

Bread

Accompaniments:

Sour gherkins

French mustard

Light red wine

Salad

Cheese

Fruit

FISH

51

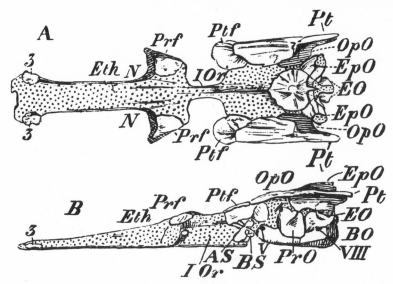

Cartilaginous Cranium of the Pike (*Esox lucius*), with its intrinsic ossifications.

JOHN KEATS ♌ PIKE PIQUED I have in mind a feast for a penurious family of five, but it is absolutely essential to the recipe that the reader will prove to be stronger and more intelligent than a five-pound fish. Certainly this is too much to expect of most readers, but there it is. A smaller fish will not do.

Specifically, I would have you catch a pike. Generally speaking, eating a pike is one of life's more massive disappointments. No other fish is quite so tasteless. Fried in butter, or dressed in flour and deep fried, or broiled — even broiled with a butter, parsley and anchovy sauce — a pike would not ordinarily attract a starving cat. Yet this pallid meat can be an excellent vehicle for carrying other flavors. Moreover, since pike comes in large economy sizes, ranging up to forty-six pounds, a single suitably-prepared pike of weight will not only provide an evening's banquet, but will furnish sufficient leftovers for the following day's cold luncheon.

It is important to catch, rather than to buy this fish, for reasons having to do with economy, masculine pride, inner satisfaction, the necessary feeling of having violated the laws of chance, and for the culinary virtue of absolute freshness.

Having caught it, kill it. Grasp it firmly and slam its head against a stone. Don't just bump it — be vicious. When you swing the fish against the rock, remember that you are obeying a divine law that says life is maintained by the murder of the weak by the cunning and the strong. Hemingway and his adherent, Ruark, both point out how necessary this law really is, and how shooting lions is a kindness to the lions, because it saves them from the hyenas of old age. Therefore, remembering how it was when we were young and galloped lions on the lovely plains of another country, swing good and true, giving Death grace. Properly done, the fish's head will make the sound THWOCK and the pike will shudder with those muscular spasms that denote the flight of the soul.

Scale it at once. The scales are more easily removed from a fresh corpse than from a stale one. Scrub the fish from tail to head with a knife, removing the slime. Scrub well until the fish is nearly white. The muddy flavor that most people complain of about a pike is due to the fact that they have not properly removed the slime.

We are going to bake this fish, and if you would be spared the taste of string, there is only one way to clean a pike. Surely it is easiest simply to slit the belly and shuck out the innards, then to stuff the fish and lace it up, but this condemns you to the taste of string, which is not to be borne by any palate that justifiably rebels at the taste of bags in a cup of tea. But to work:

Grasp the pike over the back of the head, crushing the gill plates tight, and with a truly sharp knife, cut straight down to the backbone just behind the top of the head. Turn the fish to one side, holding the head higher than the tail so that the entrails tend to fall down and back from the knife, and continue to cut around the head, behind the gills, and behind the small double fins of the throat. Cut entirely through the meat, exposing the entrails, but being careful to avoid breaking the green gall bladder that lies along the ochre liver. Then cut around the anal opening and along the anal fin, cutting deeply to sever the gut and feeling with the knife blade along the bones that secure the fin. Remove the fin. Holding the fish under water, break the backbone by pulling the head sharply back, and pull. You hold the fish under water in order that, if you should break the gall bladder in this removal of the innards, the bile will be at once washed away. Reserve the head and entrails.

You will find that the central belly fins are embedded in a trapezoidal bone. Cut from behind these double fins toward the front, working the knife beneath the bone. Then, reaching into the belly cavity, strip out the air bladder and the dark matter that lies atop it. Wash the fish well, and put it aside. It is properly cleaned for baking.

Holding the entrails underwater, work the gall bladder free of the liver and throw it away. You may, if you wish, use head and entrails in a freshwater *bouillabaisse*, but that is another dish; it is the liver that concerns us here.

Prepare a poultry dressing of bread, butter, chopped onions, celery and seasonings.

Sautè the pike's liver briefly, if not instantaneously, in a little very hot bacon grease. A sizzle on one side, a minute on the other, and it is done. Mince the liver and add it to the dressing.

Stuff the fish. Use a piece of bread heel to patch the belly opening where the central fins had been, working the crust beneath the meat to make a patch from the inside, so that the stuffing will hold the patch in place.

Put pieces of bread heel on the bottom of a roasting pan to keep the fish from adhering to the pan. Place the fish on its side in the pan. Strips of bacon — two are plenty — go atop the fish. You may also wish to put vegetables, such as thin strips of carrots or very young peas in their pods, on the fish with the bacon. You are free to do whatever you wish in the vegetable line as long as your desires do not run to tomatoes. (Only Italians use tomatoes in cooking, and they do this because even they cannot abide their national diet of boiled library paste, which they disguise, or mitigate, with the tomato. Tomatoes kill the taste of anything with which they are combined, which, so far as the Italian cuisine is concerned, is just as well.)

Pour white wine — a Traminer or a Chablis — over the dressed fish to a depth of per-haps half an inch in the pan; place in an oven of 350 degrees. Baste the fish frequently with the wine in the pan, and cook until done. When it is done depends on the size of the fish and the thickness of the meat, certainly no more than half an hour for a five-pound pike. But anyone who cannot tell when a fish is baked has no business in the kitchen.

Serve the fish. There are some who say serve the dressing and throw the fish away, but this is unkind. Moreover, it is unintelligent. The meat will have taken on the flavors of the ingredients in a way that delicately supports and enhances them. While this recipe can be used with other fish, it is best with pike because of the pike's essential lack of a flavor of its own. A mackerel, for instance, fights back.

There are usually leftovers from a large, baked pike, and they should never be thrown away. The boned meat, and any dressing that may be left, can be added to the freshwater *bouillabaisse* made of panfish and the head and entrails of the pike. Or, the meat may be used in a cold salad, or fish cocktail, prepared as follows:

Make a thin mayonnaise (thin because you do not want to lose the wine flavor of the fish) to which you add, judiciously, microscopically-chopped onion, caper and pickles. Go easy on these seasonings and on the sauce; the idea is to moisten the flaked fish meat, not to drown it.

Perhaps the only beverage unsuitable to be served with baked pike, eaten either hot or cold, is water. My preference is a very cold dry white wine with the hot baked fish; an Australian or Canadian ale with the cold fish salad.

A virtue of this menu is its economy. Most of its ingredients cost very little, and the fish, of course, is free. The only expense is the wine, but I have observed that no matter how poverty-stricken the writer, there is always wine in his house — as though to justify O. Wilde's dictum that if you take care of the luxuries, the necessities will take care of themselves.

Pike (*Esox lucius*).

Pike, including pike's liver

(One pound of a whole fish per person)

Bread for "poultry" dressing

Butter

Chopped onions

Celery

Seasonings

A little hot bacon grease

A bread heel

2 strips of bacon

Vegetables

White wine — Traminer or Chablis

Cold Pike Salad:

Mayonnaise, thinned

Chopped onion

Capers

Pickles

DEREK HILL 🐟 MACKEREL WITH GOOSEBERRIES For each mackerel have ½ pound of gooseberries. Have a fish per serving. Remove the stalks and boil half of the gooseberries for five minutes in very slightly salted water. Remove the skins and put the rest into a basin with 2 or 3 hard-boiled eggs. (These berries must first be pounded in a mortar and then sieved.) Add a little chopped parsley, butter, salt and pepper to the mixture in the basin.

Stuff each fish with enough of the mixture to fill cavity. (Naturally the fish must have been thoroughly cleaned and boned.)

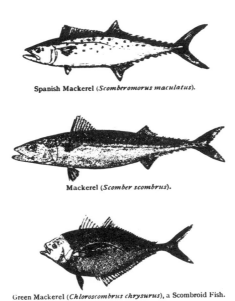

Spanish Mackerel (*Scomberomorus maculatus*).

Mackerel (*Scomber scombrus*).

Green Mackerel (*Chloroscombrus chrysurus*), a Scombroid Fish.

Put the fish in a well-buttered fireproof dish, pour melted butter over them, season with salt and pepper and cook in a moderate oven for 20 to 30 minutes, basting frequently. Ten minutes before serving, add four or five tablespoons of cream to the sauce in the dish, stir well and add any of the gooseberry mixture left over. Serve in the dish they are cooked in.

I find it a good plan to tie some string around each mackerel when the fish have been stuffed for cooking. This keeps in the gooseberry mixture. Remember, however, to remove each string before serving the fish. Once I forgot to do this and my black satin clad guest "landed" a mackerel in her lap with her fork. There it burst open with the results that can be imagined.

Mackerel

Gooseberries, $\frac{1}{2}$ lb. for each mackerel

3 hard-boiled eggs

Chopped parsley

Butter

Salt, pepper

5 tablespoons of cream

LYNN CHADWICK  MACKEREL AU FENOUIL   Coat fresh mackerel with butter, coarse salt and freshly-ground pepper. Grill, covered with branches of fresh fennel. Serve with black olives and a plate of brown bread and butter. 3 pounds of mackerel serves 3 persons.

SAM FRANCIS  ROSEMARY MACKEREL Place a layer or bed of fresh rosemary about 2 inches deep on the top of a charcoal broiler over a slow fire. There should be no red coals. Lay six fresh mackerel, heads and all, (but cleaned) on the bed of rosemary. Cook for about 45 minutes on one side, turn and cook 20 minutes on the other side. They must be cooked very slowly and very thoroughly. Salt and pepper the fish and when they are cooked, stoke up the coals and allow the rosemary to catch fire. When the fish are charred and before they are burned, put out the fire with a red wine, throwing it over the fish. This method may also be used to cook fresh sardines. The cooking time will vary according to the size of the fish. They should be well done and slightly burned on the outside. You may baste with olive oil from time to time to add richness. With the fish serve Côte de Provence wine, 1950. Serves 6.

Bunch of fresh rosemary

6 whole mackerel

Salt and pepper

Red wine

Olive oil

LEON D. ADAMS 🐟 **STRIPED BASS BAKED IN WHITE WINE** Sprinkle fish slices or filets with salt and pepper and cover with the sliced onion. Pour wine over all and let soak overnight. Melt butter in large shallow baking pan. Remove fish and onion from wine and place in baking pan. Cover with tomatoes and green pepper, and sprinkle with salt. Bake until fish is tender, about 35 minutes, in moderate oven (375° F.). Baste frequently with the wine in which fish was soaked, mixed with Worcestershire sauce. Makes 4 large or 6 smaller servings. May also be served cold.

2 lbs. of fish, slices or filets

1 large onion, sliced

1 cup Sauterne or any white table wine

3 tablespoons butter

2 sliced tomatoes, or

1 small can tomato sauce

½ green pepper, sliced

2 teaspoons Worcestershire sauce

Swordfish (*Xiphias gladius*).

PAT PASLOV ⌇ SWORDFISH OREGANO Spread cleaned swordfish with a heavy layer of homemade mayonnaise and sprinkle with oregano. Broil quickly and serve with lemon.

BLUEFISH WITH GINGER

After cleaning and washing the fish,
Rub the inside with white wine.
Stuff with slices of fresh ginger and
Sliced scallions.
Wrap in aluminum foil and bake in a medium oven.
Serve with lemon.

ROGER KUNTZ ⌇ FILET OF SOLE EN PAPILLOTE On each filet, place:

1 tablespoon crabmeat,
1 teaspoon mushrooms,
$\frac{1}{2}$ teaspoon chopped parsley,
a squeeze of lemon juice,
1 teaspoon butter, then
salt and pepper.

Roll the filets and wrap a piece of bacon around each one, securing with a toothpick. Place each filet in a wax-paper bag (you may wish to include a little dry white wine in the bag) folding the open end of the bag firmly, to secure it. Bake in a pan at 400 degrees for 25 minutes. Remove the bags carefully, then remove the filets. Broil the filets uncovered just until the bacon is browned. Sprinkle with parsley and paprika, add lemon slices and garnish when served, with a hollandaise, mushroom or piquante sauce.

ENID FOSTER 🐟 BOILED HALIBUT SAUSALITO Cover serving dish with a fresh bough thick with mature laurel leaves. Pour over leaves a large quantity of well cooked and piping hot Quaker Oats. On this place a fresh boiled halibut. This must be served immediately or the flavor of the laurel is too strong. Add melted unsalted butter.

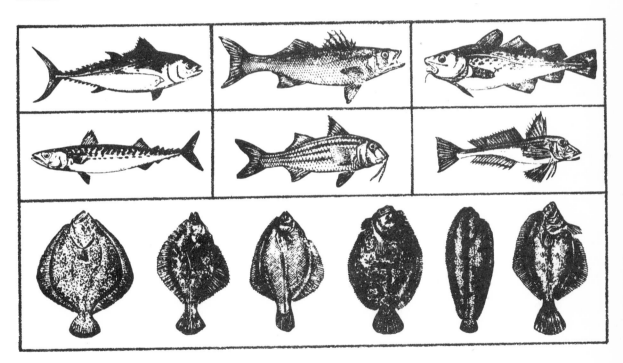

ARTHUR DESHAIES ♫ SNAPPER-PERDU

seized two eggs and broke (mashed-corn) them

bread crumbs ran out

so — used SPECIAL-K crumbled into the fragrant depths

of all herbs I could lay my hands on

including some neighbors'

sliced a bowl of peaches — mashed and distilled them until they produced

bourbon-like-nectar (then added sherry)

crushed blanched almonds

mixed their remains (white mist) with

tomato ketchup-paste-with basil-sweet-to-pink until the preparation

the color of snapper's scales

a diced onion

three onion rings thrown in like life preservers and

buoys of puffball mushrooms at the last moment, as the wave of

endless odors rose

stuff this with all to the spine right down gills to tail

with a *coup de fil* sewn up — like —

zzzzziiiiippppp — a cross-weave stitch a tailor's tack

next

swab two sides with olive oil and dust with with

flour flour (that fine wheat un-bleached and mill ground-turned-by

water-wheel-in-some-unheard-of-New England-town)

and placed on the broiler

decorated with ribbons of fat back strips

no fish was ever so gloriously commemorated

cooked for three-quarters of an hour

(a three-pounder)

and all the guests breathed   "AMEN"!!!

PHILIP HIQUILY ♫ BOUILLABAISSE *Bouillabaisse* can be prepared with almost any salt-water fish as long as they are very fresh. At least five different kinds of fish should be used and most *bouillabaisse* contains lobster or crab or both.

Clean the fish and boil the shellfish in advance. Then in a large, heavy pot place a bed of parsley. Add sliced onions, sliced or cut up tomatoes, thyme, a bay leaf, grated garlic to taste and the contents of several cans of tomato paste. Place the fish in the pot, the heaviest ones on the bottom and the most fragile on top. Add a large glass or two of olive oil, depending on the amount of fish, and saffron to taste. Add salt and pepper and just enough water so that the combined liquids just cover the topmost fish. Bring quickly to a boil, uncovered, and cook as quickly as possible, 20 minutes more or less depending on the type and weight of the fish. Add the shellfish previously boiled for the last few seconds of cooking.

For serving remove the fish and place in bowls, one for each serving. Pour the soup over the fish (or some people prefer to serve the fish and soup separately) and serve piping hot. Float croutons made of rounds of French bread fried in olive oil on the surface of the soup. Serve with homemade mayonnaise flavored with garlic and red pepper. Serves 6.

Several kinds of fish — 1½ lbs.
Bunch of parsley
2 onions, sliced
2 tomatoes
1 clove garlic
1 bay leaf
tomato paste
2 glasses olive oil
Saffron

Salt and pepper
Mayonnaise
Garlic
Red pepper
Croutons

JEAN VARDA ♌ BOUILLABAISSE A LA VARDA Combine first five ingredients with 1 quart boiling water, $\frac{1}{2}$ cup olive oil, salt, pepper, and a sprig of anise (known also as fennel, it grows plentifully in California) and boil rapidly for 10 minutes. The fish will cook up and thicken the sauce. When the sauce has boiled ten minutes, add saffron and quickly dip a wire basket with the good fish (lobster, salmon, etc.) into the sauce. Cook only enough to cook fish. Don't overcook. Place fish from basket on bread in plate and pour sauce over it.

From the remains (if there are any gourmets too full to finish the pot) a delicious soup can be made. Strain the sauce through a sieve, add water and macaroni, cook until macaroni is tender and serve with plenty of cheese on top. Serves 6.

2 tomatoes, chopped
1 onion, large, sliced
2 cloves garlic, crushed
Several peppercorns, salt
Cheap variety of fish, $1\frac{1}{2}$ lbs.
Good fish (1 lobster, 1 crab, salmon, etc.)
$\frac{1}{2}$ cup olive oil
Sprig of anise (fennel)
1 quart water

MARY HOOVER AIKEN   STIFLED EEL

3 good-sized eels, skinned and cut in two-inch pieces

3 large onions, sliced

3 medium raw potatoes, cubed into half-inch pieces

¾ pound of fat salt pork, cubed into half-inch pieces

3 tablespoons of flour

2 tablespoons of very dry sherry (optional)

Pepper

A little salt

Dry out salt pork in a large iron skillet. Pour off half the fat. Place scraps in a dish in the oven to keep warm. Sear all the thick pieces of eel 10 minutes in the remaining fat. Remove to a warm platter. Gently fry onions in the remaining fat in the skillet, adding freshly-ground pepper. Cover. Meanwhile, bring tails and skinny end pieces of eel slowly to a boil in 3 cups of cold water, lightly-salted. When this has simmered 10 minutes, drain and reserve the liquid, to which add potatoes and boil gently ten minutes.

Now the onions should be soft. If there is not enough fat left to make a thick *roux* with 3 tablespoons of flour, add more salt pork fat. Shake flour over the onions in the skillet, cooking over a very low heat. Mix well and add the eel water gradually, from which the potatoes have been drained, and stir. When this mixture is the consistency of medium thick cream, add the potatoes and fried eels and finish cooking over a low heat, with the skillet covered, for fifteen or twenty minutes. At the end of the cooking, test for salt seasoning, as salt pork varies in saltiness, and add the sherry if desired and freshly-ground pepper.

Serve in flat soup plates with salt pork scraps sprinkled over, and with either common or pilot crackers. Set the table with fish knives and forks as well as soupspoons. Serves 4 to 6.

PAUL JENKINS 🐚 CATALAN PAELLA Put olive oil in a heavy two-quart pot, grate in onion and brown. Add the *calamar* and brown quickly. Add 1 tomato, cubed, skin and all. Put in the shellfish and cook down. Add the uncooked rice and cook for 15 minutes, allowing the rice to absorb the oil. Add water covering the mixture; heat to a quiet boil and cook for 20 minutes. Each ingredient must brown separately. For grating use a medium-holed flat grater. The oil and onion is the beginning of many Catalan dishes. Potatoes and any kind of fish may be added to the oil and onion to make a fish dish. No saffron or garlic is necessary in this type of *paella* because the onion flavors it.

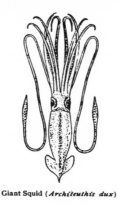

Giant Squid (*Architeuthis dux*)

$\frac{1}{4}$ to $\frac{1}{2}$ inch cold olive oil

$\frac{1}{2}$ onion

Squid (*calamar*), as desired, cut into small rings

1 tomato, chopped fine, skin and all

Shellfish as available

½ demitasse cup (½ - ¼ cup) of rice per person

Water to cover the mixture

Salt and pepper

American Lobster (*Homarus americanus*).

ELISE CAVANNA 𝔖 STEAMED MAINE LOBSTER* A properly steamed lobster is a poem of delicacy. Boiling dilutes flavor, overcooking toughens the meat. The following directions are simple, the result incomparable — and lobster is only 3.1% fat.

Have live Maine lobsters split in two, sand sack and vein removed. Your dealer will supply the kelp. Bring home as many as you can accommodate in your utensils.

In the bottom of a roasting pan place a generous bed of parsley with a little water. Pour into this a glass or more of sherry, depending on the quantity to be cooked. On this place lobsters and it is not necessary to tie the halves together. On top of all spread the kelp, put on the cover, weight it down securely to seal it, and place on top of stove using two burners. Turn up heat; when steam is established reduce heat to low — steam for 25 minutes. Serve one lobster per person. The glass of clam juice hot makes a lovely obligato to the poem.

*From Gourmet Cookery for a Low-Fat Diet.

67

Lobsters approximately 1½ pounds each

Parsley

Kelp

Sherry

Clam juice

LILLIAN HELLMAN 🦐 A VARIATION OF SHRIMP CREOLE Chop onion very fine and sauté in a very small amount of good olive oil (do not allow to brown). Add the tomatoes, garlic, all spices, and cook for one half hour, allowing the sauce to reduce on medium heat.

Brown the chicken in butter then put chicken in the sauce. Add the sausage and cook for about 20 minutes. Correct the seasoning and add shelled shrimp. Cook another 15-20 minutes. (My conviction is that deveining shrimp is nonsense.) Serve with a mound of dry rice in the center of a platter. Serves 4.

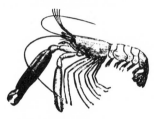

Red Shrimp (*Alpheus ruber*)

2 medium onions

Olive oil

1 large can of Italian tomatoes

2 pieces of garlic

2 crushed bay leaves

Pinch thyme

Pinch rosemary

Dash Tabasco

4 young chicken legs or small breasts

8 or 10 one inch pieces of pepperoni or linguica

Salt and pepper

$1\frac{1}{2}$ to 2 pounds of large shrimp

Cooked rice

CARESSE CROSBY ✒ TWO CASTLE RECIPES For my two favorite dishes:

First take a castle with an artichoke patch and one preferably around whose feet winds the Turano River where *gamberi* (fresh-water shrimp) abound.

You should arrive at the castle in early May when the artichokes are in bud; then they are about as big as a large walnut and may be hurried to the kitchen with the dew still on them and popped into a cauldron of fresh mountain steam. In 20 minutes they are so tender that they literally melt in your mouth. You may consume the whole artichoke, for the spines have not begun to grow — over them may be poured melted butter with a little salt and lemon added. Or they may be eaten cold with olive oil and lemon, but never with a highly-seasoned sauce — their flavor is too subtle.

Then in May, there are shrimp from the Turano. At this season tiny shrimp may be boiled, peeled and served icy cold on a bed of shaved ice, sprinkled with peppercorns and doused with olive oil, but later in the season the *gamberi,* having grown as large as salt-water crayfish, should be steamed and split open, brushed with butter and freshly powdered sage and browned for a minute or two under a broiler, then served piping hot. As this will be in July or August, you will be eating in the hanging garden above the artichoke patch and here we can enjoy our shrimp while contemplating their birthplace far below in the valley, knowing that next year and the next artichokes will bloom and *gamberi* will multiply... until perhaps some future day, *ad infinitum,* they will dine on us.

70

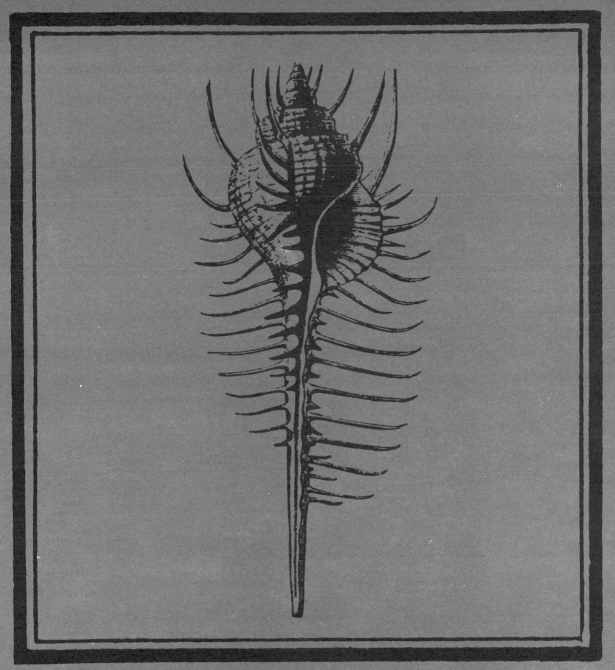

ORIENTAL FISH DISHES

71

KUMI SUGAI 🥢 TEMPURA Mix a rich batter of flour, water, salt and eggs. Use one egg for every four shrimp.

Boil light oil, not olive oil, in a deep iron pot. Roll large shrimp in the batter and plunge into the boiling oil. When the shrimp rise to the surface, they are done.

Eat with a sauce of soup stock, *shoyu,* and *aji-no-moto* (m.s.g.), to which is added grated Chinese turnip.

Each guest should have a plate in front of him, and a small dish with sauce. The cook should be in front of the guests, counter style, or the guests should be seated around the cook and his cauldron. Each guest should be served one shrimp at a time, so that the shrimp will be hot and so the cook may receive the guests' comments on the food.

Any white fish, squid, and certain vegetables (green ginger or small peppers) may also be fried this way and served individually to the guests.

Flour-and-egg batter

Salad oil

Large shrimp

Soup stock

Chinese turnips

Shoyu

Monosodium glutamate, or Accent

BARNEY WAN 🥢 CLOUDS' EARS WITH CRAB *A Cantonese Crab Dish* Soak black mushrooms in warm water for 20 minutes or until soft. Pull off (plug) the stems. Save the remaining water.

Soak black fungus (Clouds' Ears) until they open. Rinse several times to remove all sand.

Slice bamboo shoots into thin strips. (Use 1 small can or 3 small stems, if fresh

Bamboo (*Bambusa vulgaris*)

shoots are available.)

Cook the mushroom water to a quick boil. Then lower the flame and simmer. Add black mushrooms, fungus and bamboo shoots. Cook for about 15 minutes. Then add crab meat (or duck). Simmer for five minutes. Thicken sauce by removing lid, serve over rice. Serves 4.

½ package of black mushrooms

¼ package of black fungus (Clouds' Ears)

1 small can or 3 small stems bamboo shoots

¾ pound of crab meat

As a variation, the dish may be made with duck instead of crab.

SUEO SERISAWA 芹沢 BARBECUED SCULPIN WITH SAUCE Select one fresh large sculpin. (It must be large, for small ones are not tasty cooked this way.) Have your butcher remove the spines, scale and clean. Have him cut the fish in half lengthwise, right through the head. The head is the most delicious part. Be sure to broil this prized part until dry, crisp and charcoal-like.

Sprinkle one teaspoon of salt on both sides of the fish. Lay skin side down on well-greased rack over hot coals or under the broiler. When it starts to broil, pour two table-spoons of melted butter on each side of the fish and add a small crushed clove of garlic.

When the fish starts to brown, baste often with this unusual sauce: Mix together two Chinese bean cakes, soy sauce, sugar, and one tablespoon of wine, whiskey, sherry, brandy, or sake. Boil the mixture until nicely browned and glazed. Baste the fish with sauce.

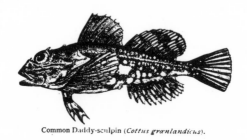

Common Daddy-sculpin (*Cottus grœnlandicus*).

Sprinkle $\frac{1}{2}$ teaspoon light-colored sesame seeds on fish. Turn on other side and repeat. Arrange skin-side up on platter. Garnish with curled orange slices, parsley, and watercress. Be sure that there are enough orange slices for each guest, because a few drops of orange juice are delicious on this fish.

1 large, fresh sculpin

Salt

2 tablespoons melted butter

Garlic clove crushed

$\frac{1}{2}$ teaspoon sesame seeds

Orange slices

Parsley

Watercress

Basting Sauce:

2 Chinese bean cakes, *Fu Yu*

3 tablespoons soy sauce

2 tablespoons sugar

1 tablespoon wine, whiskey, brandy, or sake

The sauce is also excellent for black bass, sea bass and small whole squid.

C. Y. LEE 李 BEAN CAKE AND FISH HEAD. I've eaten all kinds of delicious food, including the Shan tribe food in southwest China, such as rotten bamboo shoots cooked with fungus, boiled mountain-ant eggs, pork cooked with calf's stomach juice, pork-blood soup, etc. The mountain-ant eggs are white, almost as big as grapes; the stomach juice contains undigested straw, or green grass, a little bitter; the pork blood looks like chocolate pudding cut into little squares, swimming in sour liquid of an unknown substance. However, there is no maggots dish, as rumor says there is, although fried wasps are a very common delicacy, tasting somewhat like shrimps.

But all these dishes, although tasty, are a little too odd for my conservative taste. Of all the food I've eaten I like a Chinese coolie dish the best — bean cake and fish head:

2 big meaty fish heads (free of charge in most fish markets)

4 bean cakes (sold in most Japanese or Chinese grocery stores; if unobtainable in small towns, use potato)

Garlic, the more the better, depending on budget

Hot pepper, preferably the dried hot chili pepper,

quantity depending on taste

1 tablespoon of salt

3 tablespoons of soy sauce

Throw everything into a pot with a quart of water, boil covered for a half-hour over medium fire. Serves three to four, with rice. Coolies, serves two.

One should eat coolie food as coolies do. Use bamboo chopsticks if you have them. Suck air into your mouth to cool the burning tongue. Smack your lips occasionally. Belch if necessary. In the coolie world noise making is a compliment; it indicates that the food is hot and tasty. Good eating.

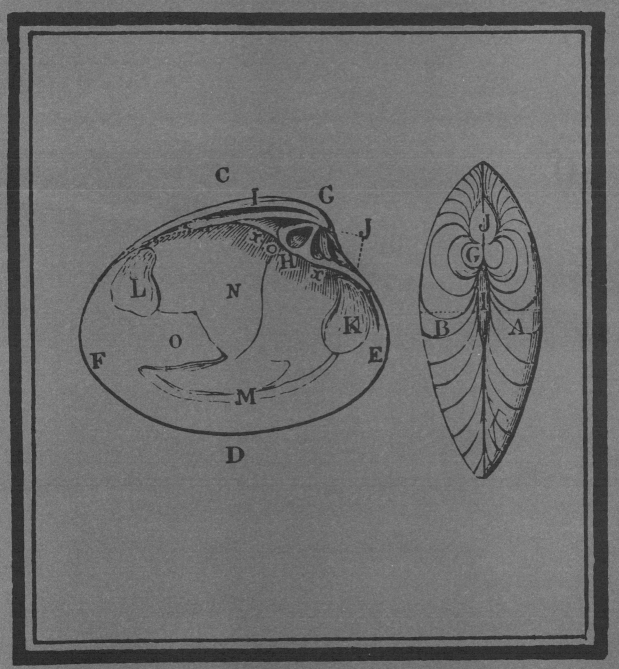

BIVALVES AND SQUID

77

ISAK DINESEN ⌇ **OYSTERS AU NATUREL** It is true that I live almost entirely on bivalves. I prefer them as they are — I think that oysters *au naturel* are as much a mental as a material enjoyment: you are eating the whole ocean.

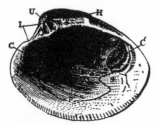

Right Valve of Clam (*Venus mercenaria*)

PHILIP HIQUILY ⌇ **CLAMS A LA HIQUILY** Choose the best cherrystone clams. Steam them in a covered pot until they have opened. Break them apart, then press one half of the shell against the clam in the other half to extract the sea water. Melt some butter and add garlic juice, pepper and parsley to taste. Pour a little of this mixture into each of the half-shell clams. Crumble stale cumin bread and sprinkle each clam with the crumbs. (Or use any stale bread crumbs, then add a few cumin seeds to each clam.) Bake to a golden brown. Prepare 6 to 8 clams per person.

JEAN VARDA ⌇ **CLAMS VARDA** Boil clams in half water, half sauterne mixture. Add butter, salt and pepper to taste. When clams are cooked quickly add watercress, finely-chopped onion and saffron. Allow to cook no more than one minute, so that the onion and watercress will retain their crispness and the flavor of the saffron will stay with the clams and not perfume the kitchen. Serve over bread which has been fried in oil or butter.

78

Fresh clams in shell

Onion (finely-chopped)

Watercress

Saffron

Sauterne

Salt

Pepper

VERNON WATKINS ♫ COCKLE CAKES (TEISEN COCOS) Welsh recipes would keep me going if I were cut off from the mainland of civilization, except, of course, that they would then be cut down to their main ingredients. I live immediately above rocks where I catch lobsters and crabs and prawns, and I have also caught in a drag net sewin, a fish like salmon but more delicate in colour and taste, which is only found here and in one or two Carmarthen estuaries.

Six-penn'orth of cockles. Stand overnight in water sprinkled with oatmeal. Wash well and boil. Dip in thick batter and fry a spoonful at a time in hot fat. Serve hot with lemon juice and vinegar. For the best flavour gather cockles fresh and avoid those with open shells. (To restore circulation, plunge hands in warm water, and slowly bring to the boil. Finger sensation has a boiling point of 1 degree centigrade.)

FELIX RUVULO ⑤ SICILIAN SQUID Clean squid, pulling the heads out and cutting to the neck. Take out the bone and clean thoroughly.

Cut in about one inch rings with scissors. Save the black bags of ink.

Slice and fry onion in olive oil. When lightly browned, put the slices of squid in the pan and cook *very* quickly until just pink. (Squid when cooked too well becomes very tough.)

Remove the squid when pink and pour red wine into the pan. Thicken and simmer, adding a little water if necessary. Break the black bags of ink and mash well. Add to the pan, heat and add squid only long enough to heat through. Serves 4.

2 lbs. small squid

2 onions, sliced

½ glass red wine

Olive oil

*Desmoteuthis
tenera.*

LIN YUTANG ⑤ FRIED SQUID Buy fresh squid from a fish market and clean out the insides. Cut the fillets into about 1½″ squares. Let drain.

Sauté celery and onions till slightly brown.

Turn flame or heat to highest point and throw in squid slices. Keep stirring contents and add remaining ingredients.

The squid cooks quickly in 3-4 minutes under a high flame. Serve with rice. For 2 or 3.

1 lb. squid

$\frac{1}{3}$ cup celery, cut diagonally (quite thin)

$\frac{1}{3}$ cup onions, sliced thin

3 tablespoons vegetable oil

1$\frac{1}{2}$ tablespoon sherry

1 tablespoon soy sauce

A pinch of pepper

$\frac{1}{2}$ teaspoon monosodium glutamate or Accent

If desired, a few dashes of Tabasco or hot sauce

JACK ZAJAC 🦑 CALAMARI AL SUGO Put the oil, carrot, celery, parsley and squid in a frying pan, with the vegetables diced very fine. Cook until the squid is browned. Add the can of tomatoes with salt and pepper. Cook slowly until the squid are soft and the sauce is thick. Serves 6.

2 lbs. squid

4 tablespoons cooking oil

3 carrots, diced fine

2 stalks parsley, diced fine

1 can tomatoes

Salt, pepper

CONCERNING FRIED CHICKEN

JOHN BERRY ∮ TOWARD FRIED CHICKEN It is my firm conviction that every carnivore should kill his own meat at least once in his life — once might be enough for a particularly sensitive and observant person to grasp the full significance of the basic act of taking a living creature in his hands and killing it, preparing it, eating it. My objection to hiring others to do one's killing is not based on the idea that one is evading a moral responsibility through some sort of squeamishness — it is painful for me to interest myself in moral problems of any kind: they invariably remind me that I survive by wronging others and thrive only on their uncertain charity. The objection is based rather on considerations of the Craft and of the Life. The craftsman should have personal knowledge of his materials from beginning to end, or his craft will suffer. I would not care to make such a categorical statement about the human being (as differentiated from the craftsman) in the midst of his shadowy and relativistic Life; under these uncontrolled conditions one could not be sure what would take the place of the old misconceptions. I suggest only that here is an important experience that is filled with aesthetic and metaphysical possibilities which must stem from a concrete action; an area of insight as against an area of inblindness. (I hope it is clear that I wish to *encourage* the eating of meat.)

I shall not attempt to outline the manifold possibilities of killing a chicken, of cutting him up in a sensitive way, exploring the points of juncture, admiring perhaps the parallels to one's own body (including the index finger and the thumb, which exist in a modified form on the wings). Why, indeed should one choose a chicken? For several reasons: he is inexpensive, easily obtained, convenient to handle, fiery but of a fairly remote connection, he has a long, vulnerable neck, and he is so inherently delicious that

I find it difficult to believe that any man or woman of good will could bungle the job of frying him.

It seems to me of little importance how you kill the chicken, as long as you get blood on your hands (where it belongs, just as clay belongs on a potter's hands and ink on an etcher's) and take care not to cause him unnecessary suffering, since that would be to introduce extraneous moral issues into a highly formal act. A sharp hatchet and a chopping-block under the open sky can be completely satisfactory. Two nails driven into the block near one edge, close together but bent apart somewhat at the top, will be handy for holding the chicken's head still while you stretch his neck across the block. Feelings of grief, dignity, exhilaration, expiation, rage, compassion, voluptuousness and the like will naturally arise in the killer, but they should not be allowed to spoil his aim. A botched beheading means a deep involvement, with unpredictable results.

A chicken freed of his head will leap and leap. This helps the victim to get the blood out of his system. It does little harm provided that you have plenty of room to dodge and don't mind the spouting. It does tend to bruise the chicken, so that you get a little more dark meat than you would otherwise. A simple way to avoid this is to hold him in a bag during his final convulsions; however, I think this is rather ignominious. When I don't want a chicken to go looking for his head, I quickly pluck a tuft of feathers from his back and lay him on that tuft, on his back. The tuft must coincide with the place from which it was plucked. After a moment he lies quietly and dies. But he must not be touched for at least ten minutes, or he will resume the struggle.

When he has stiffened a little, seize your bloody chicken by the feet and immerse him completely for about two seconds in a big pot of boiling water. This loosens the feathers. Make sure you have dipped the wings well. Throw him on a drainboard and start to work. (There is a way to make him let go of his feathers without scalding, but it is extremely wicked. Any witch will be glad to show you, for a nominal fee.) After you have plucked out all his feathers, you may find that your chicken has hair. In that case, build a big fire and poke him into it briefly, turning him this way and that. This singes away the hair. You are now ready to cut up a naked chicken. Be sure your butcher knife is sharp. Let me persuade you to cut up that chicken thoughtfully. Don't do violence to the form.

A note on waste and other casual methods: I am peevish at people who are so much at home in the world that they take its processes for granted. He who treats the world as his oyster is destined to shatter his bridgework on a pearl. (In this matter the Deity is in full accord with the Greeks.) Save the head, neck, feet, heart, liver, lungs, gizzard and fat. They're all good food. You can use the fat to fry with — it's expensive if you buy it. The other parts are excellent for soup or gravy, or you can fry them along with the rest. (I have sometimes considered those juicy pin-feathers too. I fear the spleen.)

Salt the pieces, drop them into a paper bag with some flour in it, shake them around, bring them out all powdery. Fry them in deep bacon grease that you have saved up — two or three inches of it. (Butter and olive oil cost too much. They also have a way of changing the subject. Butter makes chicken taste like eggs, olive oil makes it taste like peanuts. Bacon grease is piquant and economical and does not detract from the chickenness of the chicken.) Don't let your fire get too hot or you'll burn the chicken black; but you should have a nifty little blaze — not too low or you'll cook him too thoroughly. Try to get the feel of the process without scorching yourself in excess. The lid on the frying pan protects you; it also keeps you from seeing what is happening to the chicken. Be of good cheer. Butter is for blisters.

After about fifteen minutes the pieces might be nicely brown on the bottom. If so, turn them over. When they have cooked a while on the other side (maybe you should add some more grease?), start testing. Pull out a piece and cut into it next to the bone to see if it has stopped being pink. Smaller, thinner pieces get done more quickly than the others, so be sure to take them out first. Don't cook that chicken one minute too long, or you'll have a dry, mediocre bunch of fowl on your hands.

If you're alone, by all means lay manners aside and eat the whole chicken yourself, having fasted beforehand. It will cheer you enormously. If others are present, you must either curb your instincts or provide more chicken. (In running back and forth between the table and the frying pan, practice Zen. The chicken is in the man and the man is in the chicken. Who got there first?) All you need to go with it is a green salad and a bottle of dry, red wine.

WILLIAM STYRON ⟋ SOUTHERN FRIED CHICKEN (with Giblet Gravy)
Of all indigenous American culinary triumphs, probably the most put-upon, misunderstood, and generally abused is the Southern fried chicken which in its pure state almost no one ever gets to eat. The abuse is usually justifiable. What does "Southern fried chicken" ordinarily conjure up? To many people it signifies only memories of the great automobile routes wending southward from Washington, D.C., through Virginia and the Carolinas and Georgia, and those squat, slatternly roadside restaurants whose signs bid one to EAT (the noun-variant is EATS, and though our language is incontestably the noblest on earth, there is a raw, anorexia-producing quality in such words that makes one understand why French is the gourmet tongue), and whose personnel and glum interiors bespeak such a basic non-interest in food that the effect — were it not for the pervasive air of commerce — is almost ascetic. In such places Southern fried chicken is invariably the specialty, and similarly a travesty and a blight; there is no wonder that Southern fried chicken has received such a bad name, considering the ignominy it has undergone in these miserable establishments.

A sullen, dark scullion-maid is sent next door (it is considered profitable to run these places in conjunction with a chicken yard), instructed to wring the neck of the largest, most superannuated laying hen she can put her hands on. This she does, and then the enormous fowl is most cursorily plucked, eviscerated, and cut up for frying. Frying of course means something called "deep fry," which is to say that the owner has bought a large stainless steel vat, in which it is possible to allow several gallons of peanut oil to simmer for days on end without undergoing any significant evaporation. (It is the odor of rancid peanut oil, incidentally, that numbs the buds of smell, and gives to these places, all of them, such a gray, mercifully half-perceived, oleaginous aroma). Needless to say, to "deep fry"—to *immerse* rather than properly to fry—is not to fry at all, it is to pickle. As in the pickling process, deep frying allows for maximum permeation (in this instance, of grease) and is at the same time extremely economical, analogously resembling, let us say, the tasteless compression of frozen orange juice, or, even better, that marvel of American food technocracy which Kafka invented—the packaged breakfast cereal which is called not a breakfast food, not even a cereal, but simply "K." But worst of all is that

Seabright Bantam Hen.

this Southern fried chicken tastes horrible, it is both unpalatable and indigestible (at least that Kellogg product is not downright harmful); and one of our greatest national shames is that we have no central governing body, as the French have with Cognac and Roquefort, which might make mandatory certain controls over what could be, and should be, one of the greatest glories of our native cuisine. As it is, we have grease-soaked, old, pickled chicken, and I should like to venture my conviction that to rectify this disgrace is at the moment at least as important as, say, the winning of a Davis Cup, or possibly even a Nobel Prize for anything.

Southern fried chicken can be sublime. It is basically simple to produce, but one must be attentive and careful always. Most Southern fried chicken (I am not even thinking now of the unspeakable highway restaurants) is ruined in the home by inattentiveness, by insouciance, by the idea of — well, it's just a chicken to fry, I'll throw it in the pan. No attitude could be more disastrous, and for the production of truly great Southern fried chicken it should be remembered that at least one and a half hours of sober, selfless, undeviating effort must be spent in order to produce a satisfactory result. If this discipline be observed (and pride be taken in the fact, that this discipline must be as exacting, and can be as rewarding, as that which created a *coq au vin*), the result may be a triumph. But without discipline, without attentiveness — nothing. You *cannot* go into the other room and booze it up with your waiting guests.

First, the chicken must be very young and very tender, therefore rather small — "broiler" size. Much as one might dislike the idea of frozen meat, the fact remains that most packaged frozen chicken parts are usually smaller and more tender than those available at the butcher's counter. Certainly they are more succulent, in the final outcome, than those mammoth legs and breasts sold by the butcher as "fryers," so I suggest that unless you can get an authentic spring chicken from your butcher, you choose the frozen parts put up by Birdseye, Swanson, etc. Secondly, the covering — the carapace. There is a school, developed mainly in the State of Maryland, which holds that, before cooking, the chicken parts should be immersed in some sort of "batter." This is absolute rubbish. Southern fried chicken should have after cooking a firm, well-developed crust — this is one of its glories — but the "batter" principle simply won't hold up after pragmatic examination. The "batter," usually made of corn meal and cream and all sorts of extraneous substances, causes a tough thick shell to form over the chicken after cooking, so that there is a genuine discreteness involved: "batter," carapace and chicken interior tend to fall apart one from the other, whereas an indissolubility of chicken and outer covering is what is needed. Simple flour, therefore, is the answer — flour liberally laced beforehand with salt and pepper. I cannot emphasize this "no-batter" or "no-Chicken a la Maryland" principle enough. Naturally people should eat fried chicken in their fingers, and if you have ever been to a dinner where fried chicken Maryland-style was served, and have observed how the superfluous outer covering of "batter" pulls away from the chicken, without sense or savor, into people's teeth, you will understand what I mean. Flour — simple flour — on the other hand, merges and melds with the chicken in cooking, and therefore should always be used. But remember again that the flour should be seasoned with salt and pepper before dipping the chicken into it. Now we are almost ready, but here come the most crucial items of all: what kind of fat? how much fat? how long should the chicken be cooked?

I'm afraid that only bacon fat will really do. Crisco and its imitators, Wesson Oil, peanut oil, and so forth, will suffice, but only pure bacon drippings — uncontaminated by any other kind of fat, especially the tallowy fat of the lamb — should be used, short of the craziest emergency. I do not know why this is so, except that chicken fried in bacon fat simply tastes better — I have tried them all — and that should do, for the purposes of this essay.

As for the second question, it is extremely important to recognize that we are not deep frying; indeed, we are doing almost the exact opposite: we are *shallow* frying, and the more shallow the fat the better. This point is critical, as I tried to indicate earlier about "deep fry" and its consequences. Let us have no facetiousness when we come to this matter: one half inch, repeat, one half inch, *at the most,* is the optimum depth of fat in the pan, and there should be an effort to maintain this depth (more or less and with considerable give and take, in spite of my strictures) throughout the entire cooking process. The possible permeation of fat is at all costs to be avoided, and one half inch more or less, seems to represent a tolerable limit. (There is also a covered pan vs. open pan controversy which enters here, and is not worth dealing with: people who cook with a covered pan — "all wishfully blind," as Hopkins says — are simply not concerned with immediacy, or with the fact that the entire chicken is getting hopelessly soggy with steam.)

Medium heat throughout is best, though it may be high at the very first. There are schools which hold that the fat should be popping hot before the floured chicken parts are added to the pan, but it makes no difference whatever; I have seen superb Southern fried chicken emerge after the parts have been added to the cold fat. Practicality, how-ever, dictates that, generally speaking, the fat *will* be hot, if only because it almost invariably needs to be melted in order to cover the bottom of the pan. The cooking time itself is the most speculative aspect of the whole process. No attention should be paid to cookbooks which ordain no more than 40, or 45, or 50 minutes. Experience has taught me that a leg or a thigh, being relatively small, will usually consume no more than 30 or 35 minutes of cooking time, while a large breast may well take a full hour. Chicken livers (essential to a good giblet gravy) should take no more than eight or ten minutes. In the last analysis, the color of the chicken and the consistency of the crust should be the only determinants. The color should be a rich golden brown, and it is always better to err in favor of over-doneness, rather than that under-doneness, pale and tan in color, which can only result in a certain sogginess. Likewise, the crust itself should be firm and brittle, "crackly" in texture, and again it is better to favor a small amount of overcooking to achieve this end, if necessary. During the cooking process, it must be remembered that *constant turning of the parts* is essential. I cannot emphasize this too much. Only in this way will uniformity of color, crust and general texture be achieved, and only such steady devotion can enable one to produce true Southern fried chicken which incidentally, is best eaten with rice and giblet gravy and *always,* as I have pointed out, conveyed to the mouth with the fingers.

Giblet Gravy:

Remove the chicken from the pan, making sure that excess fat is ab-sorbed by laying parts on paper towels. Pour off all excess fat from pan, except for 2 tablespoonfuls. Add to pan: 2 tablespoonfuls of flour, well salted and peppered. Stir and cook over low heat, adding slowly: 2 cups of milk. Continue to cook, and now add slowly: 1 or 2 cooked chicken livers, finely chopped. Constantly stirring, let simmer over low heat for 8 or 10 minutes, adding more milk should the consistency become too thick. Color again is the determinant. The color of the gravy should be deep brown, and of a thick consistency, in which the pieces of liver float sumptuously. Keep hot and serve immediately. Parsley may be added, and a dash of paprika.

ERSKINE CALDWELL 𝕊 GENUINE SOUTHERN FRIED CHICKEN (with Tabasco) Have two plump fryers disjointed and soak them overnight in 5 cups of milk to which 3 or 4 beaten eggs, some salt, and a good dollop of Tabasco have been added. Drain, dry, roll in a mixture of half flour and half bread crumbs, and fry in deep fat until brown. Finish cooking in the oven, but do not allow to dry out.

Serve with baked yams, grilled tomatoes and tossed green salad. For 6:

Two plump fryers

Five cups of milk

3, 4 beaten eggs

Salt

Tabasco
Flour
Bread crumbs
Deep fat for frying

ALEX KARMEL 🐓 UNBELIEVABLY SOUTHERN FRIED CHICKEN (with Ginger and Bourbon) Actually I have no affection for the American South, which is the only South I know of that is drearier than its North. I do not like its myths or its mores, its accents or its architecture, its politicians or its preachers or its poets; I am bored by its endlessly green landscapes and whenever possible I avoid its hopelessly Anglo-Saxon cuisine. However, my wife spent much of her childhood in southern Maryland, and to satisfy — with a vengeance — her nostalgic desire for fried chicken I invented this recipe:

Chicken cut in pieces for frying

Batter made of flour, eggs, salt, pepper, garlic powder,

ginger powder, and Bourbon whiskey

Aunt Jemima pancake flour

Peanut oil

Dip the chicken in the pancake flour, then in the batter, then in the pancake flour again. Deep fry in peanut oil. Serves 4.

93

CHICKEN, NOT FRIED, AND OTHER FOWL

PIERRE DANINOS 🐓 CHICKEN DANINOS The most extraordinary of all the cooking recipes I know I owe to Spain, mainly to my Spanish. A few years ago, I was travelling through Castille, trying as usual to speak the language of the country. Having thus brought out my best Spanish to ask on the telephone, in a Burgos hotel, for the Paris exchange TRUdaine, and a number, I was provided ten minutes later with two fried eggs.

It is, obviously, too exclusively personal a recipe to be suggested. Here is another more reliable and delicious one, for people, like me, who do not know how to cook and barely know how to use the gas stove. This is the way to prepare the mellowest, juiciest chicken — all you need is:

A thick *cocotte* (I believe you call it a casserole)

A young and tender chicken, all ready to be cooked (I mean with the strings through it and everything; I do not sew any better than I cook)

A few drops of peanut oil

salt, pepper and

a good book (I don't mean a cookbook)

Time of cooking: 45 minutes.

Once you have figured out how to light the oven, put in the casserole with the oil in it. When the oil is hot, put the chicken in (it should sizzle a little) and cover the casserole. The flame should not be too high.

After about seven minutes, the first side of the animal will be golden. Turn to the next and cover. In between turnings read your book (preferably one I wrote). Then when the three sides are browned to perfection, lower the flame and let the beast cook in its own juice. Only, do not cover completely as you previously did; leave a very small opening.

Forty-five minutes from the starting point, the chicken is ready to serve. Add your salt and pepper. I doubt that you will be able to read your book with the necessary concentration. The smell coming from the casserole is so tantalizing that it is difficult to think of something else.

CORNEILLE 🐔 CHICKEN OF THE DEVIL'S FIRE Place herbs in a bed at the bottom of a pan. Put on top of them the 20 cloves of garlic which have been peeled down to their finest skin. Dampen with oil, then place the pieces of chicken on the herbs and garlic. Add salt, pepper and a pinch of nutmeg. Cover and let cook for about 50 minutes. If necessary, in the course of cooking, add a little warm water. Fifteen minutes before serving, add the teaspoon of cognac. Save the sauce to serve separately. Serve the chicken with rice or noodles. Serves 4 - 5.

1 chicken, cut into serving pieces

20 cloves of garlic

5 teaspoons of oil

1 teaspoon of cognac

Salt, pepper, nutmeg to taste

Bay leaf, thyme, parsley, tarragon, savory and

other herbs as you wish

ILSE GETZ ✍ **CHICKEN PAPRIKA WITH ENDIVES** Brown the onions in butter. Add the chicken and brown. (4 to 5 minutes.) Add salt, pepper to taste and the paprika until the chicken has a reddish color. (At least a tablespoon.) Place three endives in the pan with the chicken. Cover. Simmer for 45 minutes or until the chicken is tender. For serving remove the chicken and endives and add a pint of sweet cream to the liquid and onions in the pan. Stir quickly to blend. Serve with Persian rice*. For 3.

$\frac{1}{8}$ pound sweet butter

3 chopped onions

1 broiler chicken, cut in serving pieces

1 pint sweet cream

3 endives

Sweet Spanish or Hungarian paprika

Salt, pepper

See Persian Rice.

98

HAROLD COUSINS ♫ COQ AU VIN A LA DIDI   Melt a piece of butter in a Dutch-oven platter. When melted, fry diced onion until golden brown. Add the pieces of chicken and fry until they are golden brown. Sprinkle them with about two tablespoons of granulated sugar. Pour cognac evenly over the chicken and *flambé* it. When the flame is extinguished, remove the chicken.

In the remaining sauce, fry the strips of bacon. Add a tablespoon of flour and stir constantly while adding the wine, a little at a time. Stir until smooth. Season with salt, pepper, thyme and a bay leaf. Heat the sauce almost to the boiling point, then return the chicken to the pan and lower the flame. Cook the mushrooms apart and add to the sauce. Cover and simmer as long as possible, from 2 to 4 hours depending on the toughness of the bird. If a cock is used, it will take longer.

Ingredients, measured for four:

1 chicken (preferably a cock), cut up into serving pieces

5 strips of bacon, sliced

½ pound mushrooms

½ bottle red Burgundy wine

½ jigger of cognac

Spices, sugar, butter

1 onion, diced

Flour

MAURICE REY ♫ CHICKEN WITH PEACHES   Cut the chicken into pieces as evenly as possible. Toss the pieces in a saucepan with hot butter. Add small onions, salt and pepper. Cook on a high flame for 35 minutes, stirring from time to time so that the chicken becomes golden brown but does not burn. Pour in a sugar syrup and halved fresh peaches which have been lightly cooked in the syrup, or add a can of peach halves and their syrup. Serve the chicken with chopped parsley, the hot peach juice, and surround with hot, drained peaches. Serves 4.

Fruit of Peach (*Amygdalus Persica*). En, endocarp; Ep, epicarp; Mes, mesocarp.

Chicken

Butter

Small onions

Salt, pepper

A can of peaches with syrup or fresh peaches

cooked lightly in a sugar syrup

Parsley

DAVID CORNEL DeJONG ⌘ ZUID A recipe for preparing Zuid (Dutch for south, not related to suet, but slightly akin to Southern cooking) with explications, warnings, asides and nuances:

Explication: I am Dutch, born in Holland, was a small immigrant, hence love all things American, even American cooking (with exceptions), am a cook and take cooking seriously. The Dutch are not noted for their culinary artistry, and I want to remedy this. I like Southern cooking, even though it doesn't help segregation and vice-versa. On the other hand, the only Southern element in Zuid is whole hominy. It is accordingly possible that Zuid is vaguely related to cooking beside the Zuider Zee, in Zuid Holland, Zuid Beveland, Zuidlaren or Zuidhorn, even if electric skillets are rare in those parts.

Warning: put yourself in a quiet mood, isolate yourself in the kitchen, above all shoo out the critical cat; turn off the radio, but for diversion cook a small armadillo on the side. More of that later; its entertainment value isn't always predictable.

Nuance: pay no attention to measures found on cans. Laugh at such comments as "will serve six." Lock away all sugar, sweetenings, and flour. Take a moment to size up your guests (six) by height, heft, age, pretentions, and make an adequate mathematical guess.

Necessary elements: chicken, breasts thereof. Figure on three quarters of a pound of meat for each person. Cook the chicken in salted water to which you add pepper, summer savory and sweet marjoram. (Later you will take off skin and bones still adhering.)

Aside: the chicken is now boiling. You have time on your hands. So amuse yourself simmering the above mentioned small armadillo in a second pot. Eventually you may use its handsome shell as a disposal dish for the chicken bones and skin.

Open at least two large cans of whole hominy (if you are defeatist you'll use hominy grits) and pour off the liquid. Open at least two packages of frozen peas (canned peas are an abomination) and have on hand several slices of tart apple, several portions of red pimiento, and a handful or so of celery cubes. Also have on hand a couple of cans of condensed mushroom soup and a can of whole, pure mushrooms. A score or so of ripe, pitted olives are permissible.

Above all have a bottle of sherry. This is to dilute the mushroom soup. Never use so-called "cooking sherry." What you need is the palest, driest sherry you can get. You are about to create something delightful, not cloyingly sweet.

Also you need butter, an egg, and the spices and herbs you like. Just go by smell.

Meanwhile the chicken has cooked and has been cooling. Never mind the neighboring armadillo. Now delicately denude the cool breasts of their skin and bones. Beat the egg and drag the chicken morsels through the egg batter (no flour please) and in a skillet brown them, while you hum, if need be off-key, Santa Lucia. The chicken becomes golden brown and coherent in the skillet.

The worst is now over. Next take firm hold of the electric skillet or chafing dish and butter it. Pile the golden-brown chicken in its center, so that it looks much like a celestial Japanese mountain in a swimming landscape. Spoon the whole hominy around the chicken, daub butter over it generously, wedge in thin slices of apple and morsels of pimiento, shower with morsels of celery and a few ripe olives, sprinkle with pepper and add more butter.

Meanwhile, and somewhere along the way, you have diluted the condensed mushroom soup with the dry sherry, about fifty-fifty in proportion. You pour this solution on the Japanese mount of golden chicken, and allow it to flow like lava onto the plateau of hominy-plus. Next you take the green peas and encircle the peak of the chicken mountain; then add the mushrooms. Dot with more butter, clamp on a lid with dispatch, and start the whole business simmering over very low heat. Remember, all the contents are fairly well cooked and all it needs now is steeping, coddling, saturation, pervasion and integration.

After half an hour, or much later, Zuid is ready to serve. You may find yourself humming Santa Lucia again; all good cooks hum ceaselessly the same tune, and by this time you may become quite aware of the cooking armadillo. In fact it has been rattling sort of glassily for some time, as if you were cooking marbles. By now it is too late to do anything with it, but a good cook is never at a loss for new ideas. Chuck the armadillo into the garbage disposal, where it will start rattling, clinking and clattering even more loudly than it has been doing in its pan. Serve your guests in the kitchen, where the brutal crunching in the disposal will serve indubitably as a conversation piece.

Then, lift the cover from the Zuid, and start serving nonchalantly when backs and minds are turned because the proof of ZUID is in the eating. It is ever wonderful no matter what the distractions are.

Chicken breasts (¾ lb. per person)

Pepper and salt

Summer savory

Sweet marjoram

2 large cans hominy

2 pkgs. frozen peas

Tart apple slices

Red pimiento

Celery cubes

2 cans mushroom soup

1 can whole mushrooms

Ripe pitted olives

Pale dry sherry

Butter

1 egg

1 armadillo (optional)

Rumpless Hen.   Chela or Claw of Lobster.

PIERRE SCHNEIDER ✄ **POULETS ET HOMARDS HONTEUX**   Cut the lobsters, (which have been brought to a boil slowly in water and cooked until their shells are bright red)* into sections, setting aside the heads. Brown the pieces of chicken and the ham in a little oil until the chicken is golden brown. Then add the lobster, pour the cognac over all and *flambé*. Add the white wine, the bouillon, the tomatoes, the garlic and the spices. Cover. Cook slowly for 30 to 40 minutes until the chicken is very tender. Mix the insides of the heads of the lobsters with the butter and add to the sauce immediately before serving, after having tasted it for seasoning. Serve with rice cooked in the Chinese** manner. For 6 servings.

3 medium-sized lobsters

1 large chicken, cut into serving pieces

3 slices of *jambon de parme* (thinly-sliced, cured ham)

3 large, firm tomatoes, skinned and cut into cubes

1 large clove of garlic

Thyme, bay leaf, parsley, salt, pepper

1 pinch of cayenne powder

½ glass of cognac

2 glasses of white wine

1 glass of bouillon

4 teaspoons of olive oil

¼ pound of butter

*The original recipe indicated that the lobsters be cut up alive, then cooked in oil until the shells were bright red. To the editors, this seems too brutal to advise. They may be brought slowly to a boil or plunged quickly into boiling water, then sectioned.

**See Chinese Rice.

EVAN CONNELL ℌ PAELLA A LA VALENCIANA FOR 8 In a casserole you place ⅛ litre of oil and 1 onion; fry the onion and add 3 tomatoes (cut up in reasonable pieces) and red peppers (pimientos) and pepper — ground pepper, that is; salt, saffron, and 250 grams of Spanish *chorizo,* ½ kilo of pork and/or ½ kilo of chicken or rabbit, 1 kilo of fresh peas, and approximately 13 artichokes cut in small bits. Off to one side you are supposed to be cooking 1 kilo of *almejas* (very small clams) and ½ kilo of shrimp. You cook these about five minutes in a little water. Then you add this stuff, with the water, to the casserole — the casserole is supposed to have been simmering. When all is well cooked, add 1 kilo of clean dry rice and let everything boil for twenty minutes. Then you place it beside the fire. If you are trying to do this on one of those ugly electric stoves, I don't know what to recommend. Incidentally, while the shrimp and the *almejas* and the cooking water were added to the casserole, ½ litre of wine was also added. Now add fine-chopped parsley and strips of pimiento and eat immediately. Usually it's very good, though, of course, there are times when the *paella* doesn't turn out just right for one reason or another, but if you have plenty of wine nobody will care.

1 kilo of rice

⅛ litre of oil

1 onion

3 tomatoes

Red peppers (pimientos)

Ground black pepper

Salt

Saffron

250 grams of *chorizo*

½ kilo of pork

and/or

1 litre = 1 quart (approx.)
1 kilo = 2 lbs. (approx.)
100 grams = 3½ oz.

½ kilo of chicken or rabbit

1 kilo of fresh peas

13 artichokes

1 kilo of small clams (*almejas*)

½ kilo of shrimp

½ litre wine

Parsley

Red Pepper
(*Capsicum annuum*).

NATALIA DUMITRESCO 🐟 **POULET A LA ROUMANIE** Cut the chicken into small serving pieces. Wash and cut the mushrooms into small pieces. Put them aside with a dash of lemon. Cut the bacon into narrow slices and brown in a heavy pan, stirring with a wooden spoon. Remove the bacon from the pan and put aside. Put the chicken and the chopped liver into the pan and brown. Place the chicken, liver and bacon on a platter and keep warm in the oven. Brown the mushrooms, place them over the chicken and serve. Serve with polenta and a sauce of garlic juice and water, any desired strength. Serves four.

1 young chicken

4 or 5 extra chicken livers; i.e., 5 or 6 in all, chopped

1 cup of fresh mushrooms

Five or six slices of bacon

RAYMOND GRANDJEAN ♫ CHICKEN AND VEGETABLES Prepare a bouillon with onions, cinnamon, carrots, thyme and cloves. Cook the prepared chicken in this bouillon for an hour or more. Serve the chicken with assorted vegetables: artichoke hearts, carrots, leeks, etc., all sprinkled with coarse sea salt. Serves 4.

Carottes.

Chicken

Onions

Carrots

Artichoke hearts

Leeks

Cinnamon, cloves, coarse sea salt

Poireaux.

ELIZABETH FRINK ♫ ROAST LEMON CHICKEN Chop up one lemon; rub the outside of the chicken with the rind and put the rest of the lemon inside the chicken with a lump of garlic. Season with salt and pepper and cook with a mixture half of olive oil and half of butter poured on top and inside of the chicken. Half an hour before taking the chicken out of the oven, pour freshly squeezed lemon juice and chopped parsley over the top. Serves 4.

2 lemons

Chicken

Garlic

Salt, pepper

Olive oil, butter

Chopped parsley

107

ARTHUR DESHAIES ℰ WHAT TO DO WITH A CHICKEN THAT WAS NEVER MEANT TO BE EATEN ℰ ℰ ℰ ℰ ℰ ℰ ℰ ℰ ℰ ℰ ℰ

Place: Mexico

Purchase, barter or trade, from or with any small Mexican boy who will catch it for you,

1 stray chicken,

an outsider, self-raised (self-taught) by long years of deprivation, toughened by chance survival and whose daily rations have consisted of gravel, bits of lava finely-ground, huge flies of every species, assorted insects, corn specks twisted with the wind and chased several miles and, an approved delicacy eaten in weariness yet joy, human and animal leavings carelessly strewn about and baked by the sun, stars and moon.

A chicken whose only consolation in misery is to remain free, uncooped, to roam about escaping, by the narrow flicking of the last tail feather, death by dust, death by screeching tires, death by ox hoof or by the trampling of thousands of tourist feet. One chicken, the proudest of the lot, dingy, defeathered, toughened, quick, curious, yet who adds, mellowed by the earliest of sunrises, a melody never so cackled: cluckety, cluck, cluck, cluck.

Caught.

After a final rinsing with tequila, the old bird is stuffed firmly with a loose *paté* of mangoes, papayas, oranges, red bananas and shredded coconut, blended with a paste of lime and avocado. The bird is sewn, then drenched with a sauce of *pulque* and honey butter for several hours. Finally, in the oven, he is baked and basted until a golden brown.

Glorious.

PIERRE SOULAGES ℰ CHICKEN IN CLAY Clean but do not pluck a fat, young chicken. Sprinkle with salt and pepper. Pack the chicken in clay and bake. When the clay is broken with a hammer and removed, the feathers will come off with the clay.

108

ALEX KARMEL ♪ IMPROVED THANKSGIVING TURKEY What with the weather, the company, and the indecently early launching of the pre-Christmas season — a good time to leave the country — Thanksgiving is hard enough to take even without the traditional bird. This is a non-traditional bird which, served with either a light red wine or a white that is neither sweet nor dry, I have found effective consolation for everything else.

A turkey

Olive oil (good quality Italian or French)

Wild rice

Canned Spanish artichoke hearts

Madeira or Marsala

Moderate seasoning of salt, garlic, fennel seed, chives,

sage, mace, white pepper

Lots of chopped parsley

Boil the rice for twenty minutes until it is tender but not mushy. Meanwhile, slice the turkey giblets and fry them in olive oil in a small saucepan. When they are thoroughly brown, remove them to a chopping bowl and chop fairly fine. Swash the saucepan with Madeira or Marsala. When the rice is done combine it with the chopped giblets and parsley, the oil and wine from the saucepan. Season it moderately.

Rub salt and garlic powder inside and outside the turkey. Fill the turkey with the stuffing. Roast it in a 350-375° oven. Do not overcook. (I like the white meat still tinged with pink.)

When it is done, make a gravy in the roasting pan using flour and more wine.

SLOAN WILSON ♫ COOKING YOUR GOOSE When it comes to doing my own cooking, my favorite dish is roast goose. This is an especially attractive dish if one raises geese oneself, for they are filthy birds which attack children, and one can kill them with more joy than guilt. Roast goose means one less menace in the back yard, so the project is always a success from the start.

One does not cook a goose in the same way that one cooks a chicken or a turkey, or any other bird that I know of. Most poultry can be put in the oven and more or less forgotten until brown, but the goose needs constant attention, for he exudes grease at such a fantastic rate that the roasting pan fills as fast as a stove-in boat. If one wants roast goose and not goose boiled in grease, one has to keep bailing. This is made difficult by the fact that goose, fat and pan are of course — smoking hot and extremely slippery. Goose grease is like nothing else in the world — it's a kind of liquid hostility drained from the depths of a goose's evil nature. I have never yet been able to find a way of draining the goose grease without burning myself or spilling it. Once spilled, goose grease quickly covers an entire kitchen. Linoleum is turned into a substance which makes glare ice seem gritty. Nothing will take it off, and no one can walk on it without falling. The only thing to do is to lock the kitchen doors, and flee to a restaurant.

That's why I love roast goose — it obviates the necessity of cooking at home. It drives one to the only civilized place to eat, which is a good restaurant. There, with one's wife rested and untroubled, one can choose any of the best dishes in the world without ever soiling one's hands.

GAME

111

JOHN KEATS ⟟ COLD COMFORT II WILD DUCK Not far from our island there is a marsh, and to this marsh the turning year brings duck. One year, disaster struck, in the form of two American sportsmen who could not distinguish between wild rice and deep center field. Wherefore, to the infinite disgust of the local Indians, indigenous sportsmen and poachers like myself, the two sports baited a marsh of wild rice with corn. This drew the attention of the local game warden, who, not content with confiscating the shotguns of the Americans and hauling them off before Mr. Justice Error, declared the entire marsh off limits to everyone, and destroyed the bow nets I had arranged on the premises. But let us assume a normal year — one with no visiting sportsmen. We shall have duck for dinner.

I regard it as footless to crack the ice from one's eyelids before dawn, to shiver into oilskins, and then to sit in a freezing sump squawking like a duck into the darkness while holding a gun. Moreover, shotgun shells cost money, and once you know that you can hit a bird on the wing, there is no point in repeating this accomplishment. Not when it is

Mallard (*Anas boscas*).

far easier to set traps in the warm golden light of afternoon the day before, and not, particularly, when shooting ducks subsequently requires the spitting out of the shot. With my method, you avoid all this, and you also need pay no hunting license, because it is illegal to set traps for wildfowl. Space prohibits my describing a bow net in detail; read any good work on falconry. The important thing is to make a trap, set it, and subsequently collect the protesting proof of your cunning. Wring their damned necks. There

112

are those who claim it best to hang the birds by their feet, append a weighted can to the lower beak by means of a wire, and slash their throats, collecting the blood for subsequent use. If yours is a macabre turn of mind, and if you have a use for duck's blood, presumably in a ceremony involving a crossroads and midnight, go ahead. But I'd make short work of them, because much must be done before hoar frost begins to form as the last light vanishes.

We stuff wild ducks with applesauce (made from the fall's first fruits) and sweet potatoes, mashed together. The virtue of this combination is that it takes the wild rank flavor into itself, adding only the flavor of apple to the game flavor, now delicate, of the birds. You may, I suppose, eat this dressing, although we do not. In the cooking, it becomes an epic of grease. While the stuffed ducks are preparing themselves in the oven, create a wild rice dish. After boiling, dry the rice thoroughly, and add thereto the necessary bits of chopped onion and celery and thin-sliced mushrooms, seasoning as you will, and then saute all this in a modicum of bacon fat. The Chinese are absolutely correct to fry rice, and wild rice, too, submits well to shanghaiing.

A bread sauce, please. This is none other than the well-known graveyard stew. Milk, butter, a touch of sugar, paprika, salt, and bread. The bread is pulled into coarse pieces, which then sop in the liquid. At the end, the consistency should be a substance too thin to plow and too thick to drink. The peculiar virtue of bread sauce served with game is that it magically cleans the palate for the next bite. It has a strange, cool taste, which somehow gently underlines the game flavor without becoming a real taste of its own; convinces you that you have room for more; prepares you for a feast by leading you to believe that the feast will never end, and that there is no reason why it should.

At this point, I suggest a heresy. Surely, everyone knows that with wild duck the thing to do, to cut the oil and the wildness, is to break out the ice-cold Chablis; the Rhenish. But regard — it is cold. It is twenty degrees colder than a well-digger's fundament. The north wind blows through the walls of our house, and spills into the living room where we eat in sweaters before the roaring fireplace. Even the Quebec heater, charged with coal and placed against the north wall, does not defeat the wind that blows. A cold wine with a hot bird is no doubt fine in the temperate zone of radiant heating and but-lers, but it is nowhere on this rock in the wind. Wherefore, with the roast duck, a hot, spiced wine.

We make it, I suppose, in the usual way. A quart of orange juice, a couple of quarts of red wine, a syrup of sugar, lemon, cloves, cinnamon sticks and nutmeg added to the mixed fruit juice and wine — the whole brought to a point below boiling and then served in mugs. Balance the orange juice and the wine as you will, but in any event, when the guests come up the hill half-congealed from the trip across the windy, icy water, you meet them with steaming mugs of mulled, spiced wine and one of them should appro-priately say, "My God, it's hot as love." And so it is. And, curiously, on a cold enough night, it goes marvelously well with the duck, wild rice and the bread sauce, drowning no taste, as you might well suppose it would.

Two birds apiece for every person; plenty of rice, sauce, a gallon of wine for every four guests — a leisurely meal before the fireplace. It is time for a tart green salad — heavy on the vinegar, light on the oil, easy on the dry mustard, a bit more salt than usual, about the same amount of pepper you normally use, a pinch of a bouquet of herbs. The purpose of the salad is not medicinal. I do not believe in balancing meals, but instead, balancing the month, or year. The salad is to slowly take away, as a wench clearing plates, the food and wine. It is to prepare everyone for the conversation, which is the indispensable course of any dinner. The conversation is served with Oka and cognac.

Oka is a smelly cheese made in a monastery in Le Province de Quebec. An English-man once opened one in a close London room, and one of his guests gasped, "What is that?" "A cheese," the host said. "Made, I believe, by the skunks of Quebec." It is a super *Liederkranz* crossed with an excellent *Limburger* with a trace or so of *Port-Salut*. It is best served on buttered bread, or on buttered, unsalted crackers. The Grand Marnier, so appropriate with duck, is too sweet, of course, for this cheese. Moreover, cognac is not only more appropriate with the cheese, but is cheaper. At any event, after the pleasures of the duck and the wine, now a haunting memory because of the intervention of the salad, cheese and brandy and conversation by the fire is a fitting end for the day. Guests, like certain foods, should be kept overnight. Moreover, it would be cruel to shove them off the island into the night wind and freezing spume. Linger, to a good hour, over the cheese and cognac while the oak turns to coals; tell stories and digest, and let the coming winter snore about the house.

Bow net trap (skillfully produced after reading any
good work on falconry)
Wild ducks (caught thereon)
Stuffing of applesauce and sweet potatoes
Wild rice dish with chopped onion, celery, mushrooms, seasoning
Bread sauce of milk, butter, sugar, paprika, salt, bread
Hot, spiced wine, made with orange juice, red wine, sugar,
lemon, cloves, cinnamon sticks, nutmeg
Tart green salad with dressing of vinegar, oil, dry mustard,
salt, pepper, bouquet of herbs
Oka (a cheese)
Cognac
A fireplace (roaring)
Conversation (stimulating)

———

JOAN NEUHOF ♫ WILD RABBIT WITH PRUNES AND CHESTNUTS Marinate the cut-up hare for at least 3 hours in the wine in which have been put the carrot, onions, salt, pepper, thyme, bay leaf and parsley. Dry the pieces and roll in flour. Heat olive oil in a pan and brown the meat. Then add the cognac and *flambé*. Strain the marinade and add to the meat in the pan. Add the onions, bacon, rosemary, salt and pepper.

Cover and cook another two hours or until tender. Just before serving, add the blood and the liver, mashed through a sieve or with a fork. Add the prunes and serve with croutons of toasted, sliced French bread. Sauce should be thick. Serves 4.

American Varying Hare (*Lepus americanus*).

1 wild rabbit, the blood to be kept apart. (A little vinegar
in the blood will help it keep.)
1 pound chestnuts, roasted and shelled
½ pound prunes, presoaked for several hours
½ pound lean bacon, blanched and cooked
(blanched by cooking in a little boiling water until the
water evaporates. Then cook as if frying.)
1 bottle good dry, white wine
1 carrot
1 onion
1 glass of cognac
Salt, pepper, rosemary, bay leaf, branch of parsley
Flour
Olive oil
10 little onions, glazed (glazed by cooking on a low fire in
butter and sugar, adding a bit of water or bouillon)

PIERRE SOULAGES 🐗 **WILD BOAR** Clean the boar and season with salt and pepper, both outside and inside, pouring a glass of red wine inside. Sew the boar up *in its skin*. Use an open fire. When there are strong, glowing embers, bury the boar in them and let it cook about 18 hours. (If it is left overnight, it will be ready to eat the following midday.) When done, remove the skin, which will be hard like leather (the fur will have burned off), and serve the cooked boar with a hearty red wine.

SIDNEY PETERSON 🐗 **SEAL, DESERTERS' ISLAND STYLE** The preparation of this regional delicacy is simplicity itself. First, catch a seal (hair seal, common in the coastal waters off British Columbia). Save nose for bounty. Skin. Carve fat into strips and lay on grill over fire. Reduce to crackle. Disjoint remains. Slice liver. Broil. Salt and garnish with crumbled dried seaweed. Serve with potatoes, lemon and dry white wine, well-chilled. An alternative method is stewing. Onions are optional.

Bearded Seal (*Erignathus barbatus*).

SIDNEY PETERSON 🐗 **FIELD TURTLE** This small creature may be encountered while driving along a highway. It may easily, in passing, be mistaken for terrapin. Take home and prepare as though it were. This takes hours. Before removing from shell, examine carefully. It is a rare and horrible sight. Disengage and slice. Sauté in butter with capers. Cook rice. Discard turtle and serve rice. This will teach you never to pick up a small turtle on a highway.

In cooking, nothing is more important than learning from your mistakes. When you

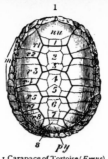

1. Carapace of Tortoise (*Emys*), dorsal surface, outside. The heavy lines indicate the divisions of the epidermal plates or scutes forming the tortoise-shell; the light lines show the sutures of the bony plates underlying and supporting the shell. 1–8, expanded neural spines of vertebræ; *r*1–*r*8, expanded costal plates of ribs; *nu*, nuchal plate; ginal plates.

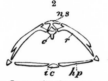

2. Cross-section of Carapace and Plastron of Tortoise. *c*, centrum of a vertebra; *ns*, its expanded neural spine; *r*, expanded rib, forming one mass with a lateral scute and ending at a marginal plate; *ic*, interclavicular scute, or entoplastron; *hp*, hyosternal scute, or epiplastron.

can learn from other people's mistakes you will learn faster. There are so many more of them. The drama is devoted to human error. Fiction has battened on mistakes, mostly marital, for centuries. Only the literature of the kitchen is entirely devoted to perfection. I think this is unfortunate. Where are the Zolas of Cuisine? The Freuds? The Cézannes? We need a "Manual of Bad Cookery" desperately. There is no virtue without sin. Good dishes derive from bad. How long did it take Rome to build up to an Apicius? More than a day, surely. Most people have the wrong idea about the history of nourishment. They still think in terms of battles and generals, kings and courts, Chicken à la Marengo and the contributions of Marie de Medici to the Grand Style. As an ever larger part of the race moves forward into an age of distinguished mediocrity in cans and freezers, the need for such a "manual" becomes more and more urgent. It will be a guide not only to nutritional sin but to creativity.

Gastronomically speaking, we wallow in a sea of restrictive legislation. Where would chemistry be today if it had stayed in the recipe stage? Where cooking still is. Where alchemy was. Such a manual would include a section on the pathology of omnivorous consumption. It would include a chapter on the decline and fall of bread over the last two thousand years. (This has already been done by Dr. Maurizio in his *Histoire de l'Alimentation Végétale,* a work which should long ago have been translated into English.)

It would include anecdotes of the strange food habits of the great and near great. It would take a good look at the actual eating habits of ordinary men and women in the several parts of the world. It would raise questions such as are apes really frugivorous? How bad was Mom's pie? What is the worst way to make a rabbit? It might even explain the following recipe which I concocted some years ago. I jotted down a list of ingredients but neglected to say what to do with them. The list follows: 2 fryers (large), carrots, turnips, onions, 4 cloves, 2 bananas, one apple, 1 can bouillon, 1 cup of apple brandy, water, pint sour cream, savory, coconut, butter for browning chicken, oil, garlic, etc.

FREDERICK FRANCK ∫ COQUILLE CROCODILE 1. *Availability and catch.* Take a crocodile-infested river, choose promontory or log on which to sit. Carefully dangle big toe in water. Look insouciant. Keep dangling. In right hand have harpoon, knife or shooting iron ready. When crocodile appears and smiles, smile back. This will make him smile in turn more broadly. Introduce implement or explosive charge into center of smile (do not forget to withdraw toe to above water level). Drag deceased crocodile onto riverbank, gather (independent) natives, offer them entire crocodile except tail

(Western gourmets despise all but tail). ᔌ 2. *In the kitchen.* Peel tail (skin to be retained for evening shoes). Dice meat. In skillet: heat a little oil, add half of a shredded onion, a little garlic and parsley. Brown lightly. Add cubed tail and cook until tender. It will look like a chicken similarly treated. Add thyme, salt and pepper to taste and sherry or white wine (half a glass). Let simmer for six more minutes. Add one can of undiluted celery soup. Mix and simmer a few minutes longer adding sherry to taste, also some mushrooms, and a dash of Tabasco. ᔌ 3. Scoop mixture into large scallop shells (available on any decent beach or otherwise in the gourmet section of department stores). Cover shell with bread crumbs and grated cheese and put under grill until brown. Serve with self-assurance.

FREDERICK FRANCK ᔌ PATE CROCODILE 1. *Availability and catch.* See preceding. ᔌ 2. *In the kitchen.* Peel tail (same) and dice but into much smaller fragments. In skillet: heat a little oil, add shredded onion, parsley, a little shredded carrot, garlic, thyme, dill, pepper and salt. Simmer for 10 minutes. Add one can of liver *pâté* or liverwurst (this saves a lot of bother because otherwise one has to go out, obtain and prepare an animal or human liver for the purpose). Cook and stir with a wooden spoon for 20 minutes. ᔌ On the side: soften 1 envelope of gelatine in half a cup of sherry or white wine. When softened add half a cup of boiling water. ᔌ Fold the gelatine mixture into the contents of the skillet and let cook for a few minutes. Pour into a mold (lightly buttered). Cool in refrigerator for about three hours. ᔌ 3. Unmold and serve on platter garnished with tomato slices and parsley with toasted French bread.

Remarks: Should the crocodile be out of season, or otherwise hard to obtain, it can be very successfully replaced by: alligator, scallops, canned tuna or salmon for the first recipe. For the *pâte,* one can take almost anything meaty: chicken, hamburger and if you are hard up and still want to cut an elegant figure take a can of corned-beef hash and keep quiet about it.

P.S. Should the crocodile omit the smile and sever big toe, simply shoot and mix big toe into mixture. In some cases it has been known to improve the flavor.

120

LABSCOUSE AND OTHER POTPOURRI

HILAIRE HILER ♪ KAY BOYLE
LABSCOUSE
OR
LOBSCOUSE
OR
BURGOO
OR
MULLIGAN
OR
POTLUCK
OR
ESTOUFADE DE VARIA
OR
PUCHERO
OR
ETC.

LOBSCOUSE OR LABSCOUSE: Of Norwegian origin, originating on sailing ships where the cook used everything left in the galley just before reaching port. ♪ labscouse, also lobscouse (181) [*Cf.* Loblolly] *Naut.* A combination of meat with vegetables, ship biscuit, etc., usually stewed, sometimes baked. ♪ loblolly [*Cf.* Lob] Thick gruel. ♪ lob, or lub. A dull, heavy person. Something thick and heavy. ♪ burgoo or burgout. A kind of oatmeal pudding or thick gruel used by seamen. A savory stew or thick soup containing meat and vegetables, orig. served at barbecues and picnics. ♪ mulligan (origin obscure). A stew of vegetables, meat, etc., used originally by tramps. Slang, U.S. ♪ Foregoing from Webster's New International Dictionary. ♪ lob, dip, frisk or pinch or sneak a. To rob from a till: from ca. 1810. Lob, go on the. To go into a

122

shop to get change for good and then secrete some of the change. 1750-1820. Loblolly is seamen's expression for steward, also for a spiritless boy at sea. Both derived from loblolly: gruel. Lobscouser: a sailor. ℑ Foregoing from Partridge, Dictionary of Slang.

Among artists: a collection of parate (as opposed to disparate) materials put into the pot for luck. ℑ The nautical Lobscouse *always* contained ship's biscuits. The false or pseudo "Artists' Labscouse" contained anything contributed which the cook of the evening decided was appropriate. Three hours are required for the cooking, and the only hard and fast rule is to put in the pot first those things which take the longest to cook.

Hale Woodruff's version, cooked on the beach at Bouche-de-Loup, boasted 37 ingredients. Some of the 37 ingredients he used were: sausage, garlic, tomatoes, chickpeas, macaroni, beef and horse beans. By the nature of the dish, it must be composed of everything left over in the house of everyone in the neighborhood.

NATHANIEL BENCHLEY ℑ AD LIB COOKING If I were to ad lib some gastronomic situation, it might go something like this:

Suppose that, carried away by the good will of the cocktail hour, you invite two friends to stay on to supper, a supper that you and your wife (or husband) has decided would be a simple one — say, roast-beef hash and warmed-over peas, preparatory to an early bed and a good night's sleep. This menu is obviously out the window, along with the rest of your plans, so you start fresh with what happens to be in the house, plus any additional items that can be supplied by the delicatessen. First off, you start some butter warming in a pan. No matter what you're going to cook, the odds are eight to three that it's a good idea to start by melting some butter. Then dice up a couple of shallots or an onion and add that to the butter, just for flavor. So far, the dish can go in any direction, but the time is close when you're going to have to commit yourself. It can either be a cream sauce or a spiced gravy, depending on what's going to go in it. Looking in the refrigerator, you find that you have some leftover swordfish and the leg of a fried chicken, and these would seem to indicate a cream sauce, so you add a little milk to the melted

123

butter and scatter in some flour to start it thickening. Then break up the swordfish and mince the chicken and throw them in, along with any similar items you may have in cans or jars, such as shrimp, tuna fish, boned chicken, or lobster or crabmeat. Mushrooms, either canned or fresh, will be a help, as will some diced green pepper and the leftover peas. Depending on how much food you throw in, the sauce will have to be increased to maintain the proper consistency, and in order to avoid the tedium of a straight milk-and-flour mixture you can add dollops of sherry and Parmesan cheese, tasting every now and then to see how things are coming. There are several ways of serving the final result: you can put it in a casserole and cover it with a breadcrumbs-and-grated-cheese crust, you can spoon it out over slices of boiled ham on toast or muffins, or you can put it into pastry shells — which are an unlikely although not impossible thing to have lying around the house. Serve immediately, with a chilled white wine and thin-sliced black bread. Follow with coffee, liqueurs, cigars, and an early bed the following night.

GWEN STONE 🦁 IMBRACIOLA This recipe was born of polite necessity in the Castello Sant'elmo, county of Salerno, the town of Padula. My father's mother, as a young girl, dominated her family, including the servants. Wars had drained the family's wealth and little remained by the Castello. Late one afternoon, visiting nobility arrived, obviously prepared to stay for dinner. Grandmama hated their guts but saving face was something else again, so she informed the cook she was to prepare a dish to delight and astound the distinguished guests. The cook frantically announced that all she had planned was some meat cooked in tomato sauce to be chopped fine over *pasta*. This was too simple a dish and would not do for the guests, thought Grandmama. So she donned an apron, instructed the cook to gather every available ingredient the kitchen had to offer and follow her instructions. The result — pure magic — and I offer it to you to enjoy with your very best Chianti.

Four slices of top round. Have your butcher pound it flat. Spread meat with shortening. Sprinkle salt, pepper, fine bread crumbs, freshly-grated Parmesan cheese, chopped parsley, small slivers of salame, hard-boiled egg chopped fine and small pieces of raw tomato — over this sprinkle small amount of garlic hashed fine. Then roll up, tie securely with string. Brown in frying pan in olive oil while humming an aria from a Verdi opera. Then, place the rolled meat in your ragout sauce which has been simmering on the stove and cook for two hours very slowly. Take out, cool, remove string and reheat. They can be served whole or in slices with, of course, *pasta*.

4 slices of top round (pounded flat by your butcher)
Shortening
Salt
Pepper
Fine bread crumbs
Freshly-grated Parmesan cheese
Chopped parsley
Small slivers of salame
Hard-boiled egg chopped fine
Small pieces of raw tomato
Garlic hashed fine
Olive oil
A ragout sauce

LOUIS UNTERMEYER 🎵 JAMBALAYA UNTERMEYER Some gourmets may devote hours to *Lapin au Vin Blanc*, ransack the Riviera waterfronts for *velouté* of Mussels, or give their souls for *Patlidjanliguverjin Kesartma*, which is Levantine for Roast Pigeon with Eggplant.

But I myself am a stew man. The household run by my wife with me — I run interference — is a fairly simple one. It is also run on rather punctual lines. I cannot say the same for our guests. Seven o'clock (my favorite hour for dinner) means seven o'clock to me. Most of our guests, however, regard this as a purely fanciful integer of time. If they arrive half an hour late, they consider themselves early.

This is one reason why I am addicted to dishes which can be prepared in advance, taken off the stove, put back again, and so on, *ad infin*. Some day I plan to write a cookbook which, as far as I know, has not yet been devised. It will be called THE STEWING HOST'S BOOK OF STEWS.

Meanwhile, here is one of the future entries. It is called JAMBALAYA UNTERMEYER. (Jambalaya is a corruption of *Jambon, la-ya — ya* being African for rice. It is a Creole dish.) Method: brown onions in butter; add tomatoes, salt, pepper, bay leaf, and fry. Add dry rice (brown, but *not* wild rice) and fry. Put one tablespoonful of butter in skillet; add meat cut in fairly small pieces; cook until brown. Add enough boiling water to finish the dish so that the rice will be neither burned nor soggy. Boil rapidly until nearly done; then turn down heat and finish cooking. When rice is thoroughly cooked, add the sweet and red wine, and let it simmer until ready to serve.

Garnish with heated shrimp and mushrooms broiled. The recipe is supposed to serve a dozen — if they are not second-helpers. If they are, it can be filling for six.

2 cupfuls of brown rice

3 onions, chopped

2 tomatoes, chopped

Salt and pepper to taste

4 glasses of shrimp

½ cupful of sweet sherry or Madeira

1 bay leaf

Butter

1 pound of fresh lean pork

1½ pounds of smoked lean ham

1½ pounds of mushrooms

½ cupful of red wine — the bottom of any bottle, claret or

Burgundy, French or Californian, will do

Marmite en terre.

SHU TANAKA 🦑 A JAPANESE WINTER DISH Cut up whatever fresh vege-
tables are available, especially the root vegetables (such as carrots and turnips). Prepare
a fish paste with whatever fish you wish, (a slice of fresh tuna, sardines, etc.). Remove
the bones and knead the fish with $1/3$ the amount of flour, slowly adding water to form a
paste. Shape the fish paste into cubes.

Melt butter in a saucepan. Add the sliced vegetables (sliced thinly or cubed) and
add water enough to steam. Cover.

Later put in the fish cubes. Let it simmer during the day slowly while painting. Add salt and pepper. Serve with Japanese sauce, hot mustard, grated ginger and pounded garlic, on hot rice.

Carrots

Turnips

Fish (tuna, sardines, etc.)

Flour

Butter

Salt, pepper, hot mustard,

Grated ginger, pounded garlic

Rice

JAMES MERRILL 𝔰 GARLIC SOUP Having parted for the night over the story of the society woman who persuaded a friend's cook to tell how on earth she made that inspired soufflé — only to learn that to the mixture of butter, flour, cream, Camembert, and egg yolks must be added "about a mouthful of water" — we found, the next noon, our host and hostess still thinking it over in the kitchen. Robert made a slight apologetic gesture toward some onions cooking in olive oil. "I had to use oil," he said, "because butter wouldn't melt in my mouth. This is going to be a Spanish soup, a very *poor* person's soup," he went on, brightening. "It can also be made with garlic instead of onion," said Isabel.

Back home, the following, weeks later, had evolved:

Cook lightly in about a mouthful of olive oil *at least* one large, thinly-sliced clove of garlic for each person. Add a cup of stock (equal parts chicken, veal, and fish, or any two of these) per person, bring to a boil, and simmer for 30 minutes. Now should be added whatever comes to mind; for instance, again per person, a small cabbage leaf, a pinch of minced fresh ginger or grated orange rind, and some slivers of turnip; then, when these are not quite tender, two or three raw, shelled shrimp, split lengthwise. Cook seven minutes more. Season to taste. Before serving, one egg yolk for every two portions may be beaten with a teaspoon of vinegar and the hot soup slowly stirred in. It's rather good. People with whom garlic disagrees have been known to eat it a second time.

Olive oil (about a mouthful)
1 large thinly-sliced clove of garlic per person
1 cup of stock (equal parts chicken, veal, and fish, or
any two of these) per person
Small cabbage leaf (per person)
Pinch of minced fresh ginger or
grated orange rind   } (per person)
Turnip slivers
2 or 3 raw shelled shrimp split lengthwise
1 egg yolk (for every two portions)
1 teaspoon vinegar

Aulx.

129

130

BEEF

131

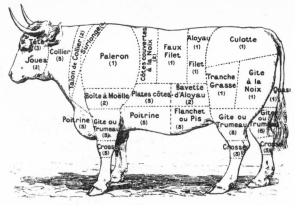

Bœuf.

EDGARD VARESE ♔ BOEUF BOURGUIGNON I consider myself more Burgundian than French and prefer my grandfather's village, Le Villars, to Paris where I was born. So here is a Burgundian recipe, with which I recommend serving *Mercurey*, a fine Burgundy, also of Soane-et-Loire. This is the *vin du pays de mon grandpère*, and I toast your health in it, and wish you *bon appétit*.

Cut about five pounds of sirloin in small pieces. Sprinkle with wine vinegar. Let soak overnight in the following marinade:

1 pint good red wine

1 sliced carrot

1 sliced celery heart

1 sliced leek

A pinch of thyme

Basil

Marjoram

Salt, pepper

2 tablespoons olive oil

132

Turn meat in marinade several times so that it will be thoroughly saturated.

As dawn breaks, remove meat from marinade, drain and dry. Strain marinade and set aside.

Put two or three tablespoons of olive oil (or the equivalent of butter) in a stewpot. When it is very hot, brown in it a half pound of sliced bacon. When bacon is crisp, remove with skimming ladle and place on absorbent paper. Place meat in pot and brown over very hot fire. Then add to it:

The strained marinade

2 crushed cloves of garlic

A small bunch of herbs

1 calf's foot or piece of oxtail

Boil hard for a few minutes, then turn down the flame and simmer for three hours. At end of this interval, the sun will stand high in the heavens, and you will remove meat from the pot. Next, pour sauce into a bowl and let it cool. Then remove from it all floating grease, and strain.

Having washed and dried the stewpot, place the meat and sauce in it again, and bring slowly to a boil. Meanwhile, brown in a frying pan, in olive oil, one large green pepper. Shake free of oil, and add the pepper to the stew, hand in hand with the bacon you have prepared, and a cup of Greek black olives from which you have removed the pits. Pour one half glass of cognac into the pot, and light. When the flame has subsided, add three-quarters of a pound of mushrooms, and let simmer for thirty or forty minutes, or until the stars are out. Serves 8.

JAMES A. MICHENER 🍲 BEEF BURGUNDY Peel and sauté heavily 12 small onions in ½ lb. of thinly-sliced salt pork. When onions are done add 12 carrots and sauté slightly. Remove onions and carrots and throw into the pan 2 lbs. of lean chuck beef cut into small cubes. When well browned put contents of pan, including all scrapings, into a casserole and add salt, pepper, bay, thyme, garlic salt, celery seed, parsley flakes, green pepper flakes and marjoram. Cover all with a cheap red wine and add 2 cups of water. Place the casserole in a 300 degree oven for 1 hour. Then add onions, carrots and 2 tablespoons of tapioca. Cook everything for one more hour. Add enough red wine to make the consistency as desired, plus a cupful of mushrooms. Cook for 30 minutes, then raise temperature to 500 degrees and cook until the consistency is proper for serving. For those who prefer more continental flavoring, whole peppercorns can be used in place of ground pepper. Drain off ¾ of the fat. Serves 4.

Marjoram.

Marjoram.

12 small onions
½ lb. thinly-sliced salt pork
12 carrots
2 lbs. lean chuck beef cut into small cubes
Salt, pepper, bay, thyme, garlic salt, celery seed
Parsley flakes, freshly-ground pepper or whole
peppercorns, green pepper flakes, marjoram
1 cup mushrooms
Red wine (cheap)
2 cups water
2 tablespoons tapioca

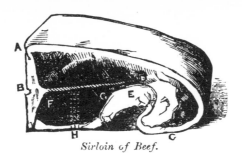

Sirloin of Beef.

S. I. HAYAKAWA ☙ SUKIYAKI CACCIATORE The name of my invention. The proper name for this dish is *o-karibayaki* (*o,* honorific; *kariba,* hunting; *yaki,* cook or broil). I have also heard it referred to as Mongolian *sukiyaki.* It is said to have originated among Japanese outdoorsmen. The simplified version I am giving here can be made with ingredients that can be found in any supermarket in, say, Topeka, Kansas. For the full treatment, with authentic Japanese ingredients, you may have to go to such a place as the Cho-Cho Restaurant in San Francisco, the only place I know of on this continent where this dish is served.

1 pound beef sliced in thin 3″ pieces (sirloin,
tenderloin, or flank steak)
1 pound chicken white meat, thinly-sliced
2 boxes fresh mushrooms, cut into bite sizes
4 bunches green onions (or 1 bunch leeks), cut into two-inch lengths,
including the green part where tender
3 or 4 large, sweet dry onions, sliced in ¼″ slices

Make a sauce of 2 cups of soy sauce, 1½ cups sweet sherry, 1½ cups sugar, 2 tablespoons sesame seed (crush with pestle before adding), 1 teaspoon monosodium glutamate.

The above recipe is for eight people, to be served at two bridge tables with an electric skillet or charcoal hibachi at each table. Four persons to a small table is just about right because each person is going to cook for himself in the part of the skillet nearest him.

At each place will be a serving of the raw ingredients artistically arranged on a plate, in the center of which is a small bowl containing about ½ cup of the prepared sauce. Also beside each plate will be another small bowl into which a raw egg has been broken.

Put pieces of beef suet or chicken fat in the skillet. When the skillet is hot, each person should dip the pieces of meat and vegetables into the sauce and cook them to his own taste. The food will be too hot to eat directly from the skillet, but it is both cooled and improved in flavor by being dipped into the raw egg just before eating. (Some people block at the idea of raw egg, but the hot food partly cooks the egg that attaches to it; once tried, most people like it very much, so it is best to have extra egg handy.)

To go with all this, people should also have a bowl of white rice and a dish of pickled cucumber. Sliced kosher dills are a good substitute for Japanese pickles.

NIVEN BUSCH ✌ BEEF A LA CALIFORNIA STREET   When I was writing Western books I used to do a lot of outdoor cooking and the recipes I liked were all for broiled wild turkey cooked on a green stick or venison roasted in the coals, but now that I have been living in and around San Francisco, the mecca of all gourmets, my thoughts have turned to sophisticated dishes and my current best, the most sophisticated and delicious one that I can think of, is Beef à la California Street.

Slice two pounds raw filet mignon or tenderloin tip, taking care that slices are not

136

more than ½ inch thick even if you whack off a piece of your hand. Into a hot pan place two ounces of butter, a spoonful of capers and four jiggers of brandy. Heat till boiling hot. Place one cupful canned or fresh shrimp in the pan and brown slightly. Just as the shrimp are browning, fold in the meat. Cook 30 seconds on each side. Remove shrimp and meat. Add cream and flour to the contents of the pan, and make a bearnaise sauce. Place meat and shrimp on serving plates, alternating layers. Place one layer of meat on the bottom, then a layer of shrimp, then a layer of meat, then more shrimp. Pour the béarnaise sauce over the whole, and serve. If you have any money left, buy a ticket to San Francisco where they really know how to make this dish. Serves 4.

2 pounds filet mignon or tenderloin tip (sliced)

2 ozs. butter

4 jiggers brandy

Capers

Cream

Flour

1 cup canned or fresh shrimp

SAM FRANCIS ℥ **STUDIO STEAK** Take a porterhouse steak that is at least 2½ inches thick and remove the bone. Dampen 10 pounds of salt with a little water (not enough to dissolve it) and make a sandy paste, mixing it with your hands. Put ½ inch layer of the salt mixture on one side of the steak. It will harden into solid. Broil the steak with the salt on top of it for 15 minutes (optional time). Take it off and put a ½ inch layer of the salt on the other side. Broil 10 minutes. (The steak will be medium rare.) Melt a pound of butter. When the meat is done, break off the salt. You may need a hammer. Dip slices of the steak in melted butter with freshly-cut mushrooms in it. Eat the meat between slices of French bread and serve with either elderberry or loganberry wine and artichoke hearts.

Porterhouse steak, 2½ inches thick

10 pounds salt

1 pound butter

Mushrooms

PHILIP HIQUILY ℥ **STEAK ACETYLENE** Take a top quality sirloin steak and place it on a metal or fireproof platter which has been greased with lard or a little oil. Heat with an acetylene torch just until the topmost layer is lightly blackened. Turn the steak and scorch the other side. Serve with parsley butter.

MARCEL DUCHAMP ℥ **STEAK TARTARE** Let me begin by saying, *ma chere*, that Steak Tartare, alias *Bifteck Tartare,* also known as *Steck Tartare,* is in no way related to tartar sauce. The steak to which I refer originated with the Cossacks in Siberia, and it can be prepared on horseback, at a swift gallop, if conditions make this a necessity.

Indications: Chop one half pound (per person) of the very best beef obtainable, and shape carefully with artistry into a bird's nest. Place on porcelain plate of a solid color—ivory is the best setting—so that no pattern will disturb the distribution of ingredients. In hollow center of nest, permit two egg yolks to recline. Like a wreath surrounding the nest of chopped meat, arrange on border of plate in small, separate bouquets:

Chopped raw white onion

Bright green capers

Curled slivers of anchovy

Fresh parsley, chopped fine

Black olives minutely chopped in company

with yellow celery leaves

Salt and pepper to taste

Each guest, with his plate before him, lifts his fork and blends the ingredients with the egg yolks and meat. In center of table: Russian pumpernickel bread, sweet butter, and tall bottles of *vin rosé*.

ROBERT ELLIS 🦟 HAMBURGER STROGANOFF Chop an onion and brown in butter. Brown ¾ pound of choice ground round steak. Add salt, pepper, paprika, m.s.g. and chopped garlic to taste. Then add a can of mushroom soup, or sliced fresh mushrooms and 1½ cups of beef stock. Add flour if needed to thicken. Cook 15 to 20 minutes. Before serving stir in a pint of sour cream. Serve on toast, rice or noodles. Serves four.

139

¾ pound choice ground round steak

Onion

1 can of mushroom soup (or sliced fresh mushrooms)

1½ cups beef stock

Chopped garlic

Salt, pepper, paprika, m.s.g.

1 pint sour cream

White Globe.

HOSIASSON ≈ KOTLIETA Take the soft, inside part (in French, the *mie*) of a half a loaf *(baguette)* of French bread, tear into pieces and dampen with milk. Press the bread until it is moist but not soggy. Add the bread and a slightly-beaten egg to one pound of ground round or chuck. Brown sliced onions in butter and add these to the meat mixture. Fold and mix all thoroughly, but gently. Add salt and pepper and shape into flat (about ¼ inch) patties. Roll in bread crumbs and fry in butter. Serves 4.

½ loaf French bread

1 egg, slightly-beaten

1 pound of ground round or chuck

Onions, sliced

Salt and pepper
Bread crumbs
Butter

HELEN FRANKENTHALER HAMBURGER HELENE *for my husband, Robert Motherwell* Take an individual hamburger patty (preferably top round and fat free), season with salt and pepper (and charcoal powder, optional). Broil under high flame for a minute on each side. Cover with a mixture of coarsely-chopped Swiss (or old Cheddar) cheese and prosciutto ham. Broil another two minutes. Place on toast lightly spread with Dijon mustard. Sprinkle with chopped chives (fresh or dried). Garnish with mustard pickle and serve with cold beer.

This sounds like a fancy hamburger but, in fact, it has another taste altogether.

Hamburger patty (per person)
Salt, pepper (optional: charcoal powder)
Chopped Swiss cheese
Prosciutto ham
Dijon mustard
Chopped chives

MILTON RESNICK CHINESE MEAT BALLS Make meat balls of the very best ground beef. Place with as many Brussels sprouts as desired in a pressure cooker with a little water. Cook.

MATSUMI KANEMITSU ⚜ FRANKFURTERS JAPONAIS

Slice and place in a mixing bowl:

One pound of frankfurters

Blend in thoroughly:

2 teaspoons of salt

A dash of pepper

1 clove of garlic, diced

1 teaspoon of diced scallion

Cook in boiling water until *almost* tender:

3 cups of fresh, sliced mushrooms

In a preheated frying pan, place:

2 teaspoons of oil

1 teaspoon of soy sauce

A dash of pepper

Add the mushrooms to the mixture in the bowl and cook everything over a low flame. Stir constantly until browned. Serve with hot rice. Serves 4.

142

HARRY GOLDEN ∬ "HOLISHKAS" OR STUFFED CABBAGE This is my favorite recipe for *holishkas*. Some Jews call these *prakas*. It depends upon the Eastern European region from which you come.

Actually, I believe this very delightful dish is Ukrainian. Up in Winnipeg where they have a very large Ukrainian population there are restaurants with neon signs, *Halupti,* and when I went in to sample the *halupti* I found that they were almost as good as my mother's *holishkas*.

2 pounds lean, raw beef, chopped

Salt and pepper to taste

1 cup cooked rice

2 cans tomato sauce

2 cans tomato paste

1 onion, chopped

½ cup vinegar

2 cups water

⅓ cup sugar

16 -18 ginger snaps

Large cabbage leaves

Chou Cœur de-bœuf.

Soak the cabbage leaves in hot water a few minutes to make them less brittle. Season the meat lightly with salt and pepper. Add rice. Roll a portion of the meat mixture in each leaf. Place them in a large low pan with the rest of the ingredients and let simmer until the cabbage is tender and well browned. Serves 6-8.

RUPERT CROFT-COOKE 🖎 PUDDING The word drops with a thud. Its cousin, dumpling, is scarcely less heavy. They, with pies, pasties and patties might be taken as symbols of English cookery.

The very names are ours and some of them have been taken and corrupted by other languages. "Pudding" is from the Middle English "poding," and sounds like it, a good solid perhaps even stodgy word. The Oxford Dictionary suggests that "pie" comes, because of its miscellaneous contents, from "magpie" while "dumpling" derives from the Anglo-Saxon "dump," (damp or heavy) and the old English suffix of endearment, "-ling." These words were being used in the fourteenth century or earlier and from that time we have delighted in the food they name.

All early authors of books on cookery, Sir J. Elliott (1539), Abraham Veale (1575) and Robert May (1665) show this with more or less emphasis and there is an ordinance of the cooks and pastelers or piebakers dated 1378. We have, throughout our history as a nation, had a weakness for meat in pastry which, while it is not unique, is a sort of hallmark of our taste. In *Piers Plowman* and John Lydgate's *London Lackpenny* pies and puddings are both mentioned with longing. Even today the older of those who "take their dinners with them to work" are in more cases than not supplied with a pastry rather than sandwiches or meat and bread.

"I think I could eat one of Bellamy's meat pies," were the last words of William Pitt the Younger, most English of statesmen, who had that touch of mystery in his competence, that odd and perverse unexpectedness in tactics which baffles foreign observers of our peculiarities. Who would have attributed to him such a sound and earthy desire at the last? So curious was it to historians that a more suitable but entirely spurious sentiment was put in his mouth — "My country! Oh my country!" But "Bellamy's meat pies" has the authentic touch. No one could have made up that — anyone could, in fact *would,* and certainly *did* invent "my country" for the last words of a great patriot.

Pies and puddings — our literature is full of them and if our art had ever been, as Dutch, Italian and Spanish art at certain times was, an expression of ourselves, an interpretation of popular and not merely aristocratic life, our art would have known them too. It is too much to ask of Gainsborough that he should have shown one of his countesses devouring a Cornish pasty, or of Turner that he should leave his landscapes to do an appetizing mural in the dining room of an inn, but the Dutch would have depicted pies with their loaves and flagons if they had been the people's food as in England they were.

Pies and puddings — how gross, how vulgar, how unepicurean they sound. Food for Dr. Johnson, perhaps, or any of the great guzzlers of the eighteenth century, food for Falstaff, food for city folk who bought at cookshops and for harvesters who carried their pastry wrapped in a red handkerchief. But food with which to challenge the strongholds of Escoffier, the truffles and soufflés of Brillat-Savarin? They certainly do not sound like it.

I am glad they are untranslatable and only Isabella Beeton with her idiotic passion for giving the French name in brackets after the English has talked of *Pouding de Boeuf et de Rognon* while even she is defeated by dumplings and toad-in-the-hole. (Why not *Crapaud-dans-le-Trou?*) *Pâté* has ceased to be an equivalent for pie or pastry and though you can talk of *Pâté de Gibier* it is not what we mean by a game pie for it has long ago lost its pastry. Surely no English restaurant which served a Cornish pasty would let it appear on the menu as *Pâté Cornouaillaise?* Certainly the French would use the English term as they did long ago with others of ours to create in time "Bifteck" and "Rosbif."

145

The foremost of them all, a lordly food, is the steak-and-kidney pudding. In this the flavour is imprisoned by the suet pastry for the four or five hours during which it is steamed, giving to the resulting gravy and meat a richness of taste and consistency obtainable in no other way known to me. I was shocked the other day when a man of some discrimination and knowledge in food said that he preferred a steak-and-kidney pie, that more pretentious but infinitely less flavoursome cousin of the pudding. How can it achieve distinction except as a stew which has been covered with crisp or flaky pastry? The whole point of the pudding is the long hours in which the meat slowly softens and blends with the herbs and spices, which must be used lightly, so strongly does everything sealed inside the thick blanket of white suet pastry keep its flavour.

Steamed puddings of all kinds are a favourite food with the gypsies, for they can be left in the pot for an hour or two while mother goes hawking, leaving instructions with the children to keep the fire in. When I travelled with a gypsy we made steamed pudding twice a week, using them not only for steak but also for rabbit and other things. I can remember the scent of the wild thyme we put in, a scent which in any other food would have been lost long before cooking was finished. Therein lies the excellence of the steamed pudding — it retains all the rich flavours which develop while it cooks. Shut in its heavy pastry, the savour and odour are released only when it is cut.

For it a good-sized pudding basin is necessary and I was startled when I first began housekeeping in Tangier to realize that the pudding basin as we understand it is an English peculiarity, unpurchasable abroad in the familiar shape and substance. I had to bring one out from home after my first visit to London and if there is ever a crash in the kitchen I tremble for it. The pudding basin is greased, then lined with a suet paste made by mixing flour and chopped suet in the proportion of two to one, with salt and enough water (not milk) to make it workable dough. Baking powder may be added but will not help it much for its leavening effect will have greatly diminished before the pudding is ready. There is a "trick" procedure here which I learned to follow many years ago, and which has stood me in good stead. Mix into the paste a very little *black treacle,* (an invaluable thing to keep in stock in any case). This will give it when cooked that slightly

146

golden colour and the suggestion of a taste of rum for which the steak-and-kidney pud-dings of a Fleet Street pub were once famous. Keep enough of the paste to seal up the top when the other ingredients are in. What exactly these will be depends on your taste and pocket. Two-thirds steak to one-third kidney, both cut into pieces of about a cubic inch in size, are essentials. Oysters are a traditional addition but not quite a necessity. Mushrooms certainly. Onion of course, which should be browned in the frying pan, as the meat should be, before going in. Herbs and garlic very sparingly; remembering that every suggestion of flavour will be miraculously preserved if not increased in that con-finement. Bacon can be tried, so can chestnuts. A little red wine improves but is not essential to the result. When all is in and the space fairly tightly filled, pour in stock or water nearly to cover it, seal it with your piece of suet paste after dampening the rim of the suet paste already in place, to form a good joint. Tie a pudding-cloth over it and steam it for four or five hours — not more.

There are many other things that can be done in the same way, though none are so good. The brain and tongue from a calf's head, bacon, a rabbit, veal, even mutton, but with these last three some ingenuity, a couple of kidneys, a little chopped ham and more chopped herbs should be used. The variations are almost infinite but the true ingredients are steak and kidney.

No Scot would let us claim sovereignty in this, however. For him the "great chieftain of the pudding race," as Burns called it, is the haggis. Glibly do the writers of cookery books give instructions for making this, ("Take a sheep's paunch and pluck") but did any of them, I cannot help wondering, ever actually do it? Or did they, as I must confess I do, buy one ready made in Scotland? This curious and delicious combination of oatmeal with chopped liver, heart and lights of the sheep, with chopped suet and onion, nutmeg, lemon juice, salt and pepper, seems to me best made by experts who understand the use of oatmeal as no Sassenach can. But you don't have to come from north of the Tweed to agree with Burns —

> "Weel are ye wordy o' a grace
> As lang's my arm."

147

It is not by the written word, however lyrically they are celebrated, that these foods of ours are most honoured, for before printing came they were spoken of in proverbs and most of all in nursery rhymes. Perhaps in nurseries still are remembered Little Jack Horner who sat in a corner eating a Christmas pie, or Simple Simon who met a pieman, or the Queen of Hearts who baked some tarts, or the four-and-twenty blackbirds who were baked in a pie, or Rowley Poley pudding and pie, or Pease-porridge hot, Pease-porridge cold. With that kind of immortality they will not easily be lost to us, whatever the attractions of fiddly little fritters that can be cooked in five minutes before a television camera or clever inventions intended to make palatable the food from tins or ingenious snacks disguising corned beef. Nor can they altogether be dismissed by prissy jokes about English cookery.

Flour

Chopped suet

Salt

Black treacle

Steak, chopped in pieces 1 cubic inch — $\frac{2}{3}$

Kidney, chopped in pieces 1 cubic inch — $\frac{1}{3}$

Oysters (optional)

Mushrooms

Onion

Bacon (optional)

Chestnuts (optional)

Red wine (optional)

Herbs and garlic

Male Flowering Branch (1) and Fruiting Branch (2) of Hop (*Humulus Lupulus*).
a, male flower; *b*, female flower; *c*, single fruit; *d*, embryo.

CALVIN KENTFIELD ❧ SUMMER COLD LOAF OR BEER LOAF This is an improvement on a buffet dish often found at lunchtime in the saloon bars of English pubs.

Make a meat loaf from any combination of lean ground meat such as beef, veal, and sausage (cook the sausage first if it's very fat); chopped onions; chopped parsley; bread or cracker crumbs; a couple of eggs; leaf sage; cracked pepper; sweet basil or summer savory; some dry mustard; salt; and a drop of sherry.

Grease and line the loaf pan, bottom and sides, with nearly half an inch of short pastry (a liquid shortening dough is very quick and ideal); put half of the meat into the bottom of the pan then lay, end to end through the center, a line of hard-boiled eggs. (Take off the shells for God's sake.) Cover the eggs with the rest of the meat and lay a lid of dough on top. Bake until the crust is brown and eat cold in slices with hot mustard and cold beer.

Ground meat

Chopped onions

Chopped parsley

Bread or cracker crumbs

Hard-boiled eggs

Leaf sage, cracked pepper, sweet basil or summer savory

Dry mustard

Sherry

Pastry

KAREL APPEL 🔁 OLD BEAMS WITH SPLINTERS OF A VIKING AXE
(OUDE BALKEN MET VERSPLINTERDE VIKING BIJLEN).

2 tablespoons water

½ cup milk, scalded

2 tablespoons shortening

½ cake compressed yeast (or one package active, dry yeast)

1 tablespoon sugar

½ teaspoon salt

1 well-beaten egg

2 cups sifted flour

First make a roll dough with the above ingredients. Soften the compressed yeast in lukewarm water. (For active, dry yeast use slightly-warmer water.) Combine the milk, shortening, sugar and salt and let the mixture cool. Then add the softened yeast and the well-beaten egg. Gradually stir in the flour and beat vigorously. Then take:

150

½ pound ground chuck

½ pound diced, precooked chicken

1 cup diced, boiled mushrooms

1 medium onion, chopped

½ cup finely-cut jellied fruits

½ cup grated Parmesan cheese

¼ pound flat noodles

1 or more Spanish red peppers, chopped (these are the splinters)

2 medium tomatoes, quartered

Fresh garlic juice, to taste

Olive oil

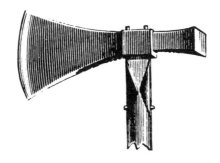

Brown the ground meat in olive oil. Cook the flat noodles *(tagliatelli)* in boiling, salted water until *al dente*. Mix the browned meat with the precooked, diced chicken and mushrooms, the chopped onion, jellied fruits and as much of the chopped red pepper as taste allows. Roll the dough on a lightly-floured surface to a rectangle ¼ inch thick and as wide as the noodles are long. Cover with the meat mixture and sprinkle lightly with freshly-pressed garlic juice. Drain the noodles and place them lengthwise across the width of the rolled dough. Sprinkle the grated cheese over all and roll as you would a jelly roll, the noodles parallel to the resulting "log." Put the "log" in a long pan, preferably the type used for boiling fish, and brown on all sides in preheated olive oil. After five minutes of browning, add the quartered tomatoes and a little water. Cover tightly and cook for 10 to 15 minutes, turning often. When done, cut in round slices about four inches long and serve with an ample quantity of cold beer. Serves from four to six.

LAMB AND A GOAT

153

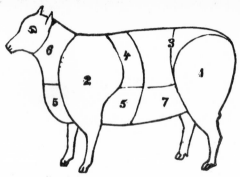

Carcass of Sheep.

ANTHONY WEST 🐑 COUNTRY MUTTON STEW I first started to cook when I lived in a stone-built English farmhouse in the Nadder Valley in Wiltshire. The house had a big stone-floor kitchen with a huge coal range in it, a larder with slate shelves four inches thick, and no icebox. The farm had water meadows running down the valley alongside the stream, and I often used to shoot wild duck in among the reed-choked channels of the old irrigation system. The fields of kale and roots grown as winter keep for the cattle used to draw pigeons in the hard weather, and earlier in the autumn before the stubbles were tined in by the ploughs it was easy to get greedy pheasants gleaning out in the open. Rabbits were to be had at all seasons. With these sources of supply, game played a large part in my early repertory. So did the art of marinading, since when you are out with a gun you do not have a chance to pick out only the young and tender creatures you would select in a shop. All pigeons and most rabbits needed marinading for at least twenty-four hours. Later on when I was living in towns and stretching my income as far as it would go I found that the marinade made it possible to save a good deal of money at meat counters since it does wonders for what would otherwise be a great deal less than the best. To make your marinade:

Place a sliced carrot, a sliced onion, and a small head of celery cut up in a saucepan with a wineglass full of warm olive oil and cook till these are lightly browned. Then add a quarter of a pint of white wine and about half a wineglass full of wine vinegar. Now

154

add a bouquet of herbs made of rosemary, parsley, thyme and bay leaf; 2 cloves of garlic, a few shallots, some peppercorns and salt. Simmer for thirty minutes and when it is cold, pour it over the meat or game needing treatment. A table bird or a good cut of meat will not need more than a couple hours of this, but a piece of stewing beef can be left to steep for as much as forty-eight hours to advantage. Some people may prefer to use a red wine for beef or mutton. When the steeping is over the soggy bouquet of herbs should be dredged from the marinade and replaced by a fresh one. The rabbit, or whatever, can then be stewed or braised in the liquor.

Marinading is the foundation of a great many interpretations, but especially fragrant and agreeable are dishes such as *Country Mutton Stew:* Take 4 lbs. of stewing pieces of what your butcher will call lamb and place in a marinade for six hours or so. When that time has gone by, dice four ounces of Canadian or other lean bacon and start cooking it gently in five tablespoonfuls of olive oil. Add four large onions, sliced, and when they begin to brown add the mutton from the marinade. Dredge the marinade and pour the clear liquor into the stew. Add a fresh bouquet of herbs, 2 new cloves of garlic, the skin of half an orange, and turn up the flame so that the stew begins to bubble fiercely and to reduce. When about a third of all the wine has boiled away, pour in a tablespoonful of cooking brandy and add a cupful of dried Chinese mushrooms (which can be found in most Chinese food stores). Now pour boiling water into the stew until the meat is covered, put the lid on the stewpot and turn down the flame so that it simmers gently for the next four hours. All that remains to be done before the dish is served is to skim off any excess fat which may have risen to the surface. Serves 6-8.

Ingredients for Marinade:
A sliced carrot
A sliced onion
A small head of celery cut up
A wineglass of warm olive oil

155

¼ pint of white wine (½ cup)

Half a wineglass of wine vinegar

Rosemary, parsley, thyme and bay leaf

2 cloves of garlic

A few shallots

Peppercorns, salt

Ingredients for Country Mutton Stew:

4 pounds of stewing pieces of lamb or mutton

A marinade

¼ lb. of Canadian or other lean bacon

Five tablespoons of olive oil

Four large onions

A fresh bouquet of herbs

2 new cloves of garlic

Skin of half an orange

A tablespoon of cooking brandy

A cupful of dried mushrooms (preferably Chinese)

DONALD DOWNES ♋ DRUSE LAMB DISH Lebanon and Syria and Jordan I like as much as I dislike their governments and their absurd international pretentiousness. I was living among the Druses in a wildly 19th-century romantic Byronic ruin of a Crusader-time Saracen castle, accommodated in the 16th century, in part, to make the serai for a Druse emir. It looks down from its peak onto the Mediterranean from Tyre and Sidon to Byblos. The village life — except for intermittent electricity — is as it

was 800 years ago. I enjoyed it thoroughly and sat long hours beside the fountain in the courtyard beside a frangipane tree under the high 12th-century vaulting and worked. In the evenings a dozen or so villagers came in to sing, play backgammon, drink arak and tell tall tales which unfortunately I could only understand in my host's translated condensations. I pass on to you a good Druse recipe for a baked dish (for four):

3 pounds of eggplant
3 cloves of garlic
1½ cups of yoghurt
1 tomato
¼ cup sesame or olive oil

157

10 black olives

2 green peppers

1 pound of chopped raw mutton or lamb

4 sprigs of mint

4 sprigs of basil (or tarragon)

$\frac{1}{4}$ teaspoon of cinnamon

Cayenne powder and salt to taste

Roast the eggplants and the peppers over an open gas flame until black. Peel. Reserve one clove of garlic, one cup of yoghurt and the mint for the sauce. Put all the rest of the ingredients in a chopping bowl and chop fine and mix. Place in a baking dish and bake in a fast oven about 20 minutes. For the sauce, smash the one clove of garlic and mix into the yoghurt. When the dish is finished, pour the sauce over the hot dish and sprinkle it with the chopped mint. Yum, yum.

ANTHONY WEST ♌ LEG OF LAMB I used to spend about three months of every year in France and made a point of going to the restaurants starred in the Michelin guide. While I enjoyed a good deal of what I ate in such places, I slowly came to realize that elaborate restaurant cooking has very little to do with what can or should be done at home. Famous recipes from famous restaurants are really not worth collecting since they call for, without saying so, the invisible resources of a big kitchen in the way of an elaborate battery of utensils and the reserves of material which can be built up while cooking for eighty or more people at every meal. I have always found cookbooks which drew on the traditional repertory of the farmhouse or the *bourgeois* kitchen much more useful. When planning an evening of music at home it is much better to try *lieder*, piano solos, trios, and quartets than it is to attempt scaled-down operas and symphonies. A sound general principle on which I have come to rely is to let first-class material speak for itself by cooking it as simply as possible, and to cook more elaborately when the necessity of inferior material forces one to do so. Here, by way of contrast with the *Country Mutton Stew* is the way to cook a tender young leg of lamb:

Rub it all over with salt and the cut ends of a clove of garlic, then insert small fragments of garlic in a few strategic folds in the meat which will accept them. Put the leg of lamb on a roasting pan with a lid and surround it with peeled and halved potatoes. Put the covered pan into an oven, preheated to 450 degrees, and let the joint cook quickly for fifty minutes to an hour, interrupting the process once to turn over the potatoes so that they will be nicely browned on both sides. Those who like their lamb rose pink should have it out of the oven instantly when the fifty minutes are up; those who like it better done may leave it till the life goes out of the meat, if they must. In either case the joint should be left standing in the closed tin for ten minutes before it is brought to the table. It will not be good if opened immediately. People who do not like garlic will ask you what makes your lamb so delicious if you do it this way. Do not tell them; pretend that the secret is in the hot oven and the speed at which the meat cooks. Serve with young green garden peas, or Brussels sprouts, and with good claret. Follow with some simple classic like apple pie with one quince sliced into it, and plenty of very cold sweet cream, or baked apples done with the cores removed and their centers filled with raisins and either honey or brown sugar.

A young leg of lamb
Salt
Clove of garlic
Peeled and halved potatoes

HERBERT ASBURY 🐑 **LEG OF LAMB WITH HONEY AND SOY SAUCE** Cut all the fat off the leg of lamb. Rub a little pepper in, and a *very little* salt. Smear all over with honey. Place in a baking pan in ¼ inch of water. Pour over the leg of lamb one half bottle of soy sauce. Bake one half hour at 425 degrees. Reduce heat to 350 degrees and bake until done, at least one half hour per pound. Baste frequently with soy sauce. There should be no grease in the gravy, but if there is, pour it off. Then thicken gravy to taste with flour or cornstarch.

Leg of lamb

Pepper

Honey

Soy sauce

Flour or cornstarch

MERVIN JULES 🐑 **LEG OF LAMB MERVEILLEUX** Seize a leg of lamb that has been boned but not rolled and dunk it, overnight or longer, in the following marinade:

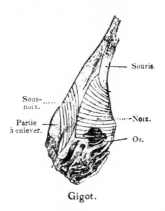

Gigot.

6 cloves of garlic, finely-chopped

2 bottles of the best French dressing

2 brutally crushed bay leaves

1 teaspoon oregano

2 cups chopped onion

$\frac{1}{2}$ teaspoon fresh mint leaves (or dried)

2 teaspoons of barbecue-spice powder

1 tablespoon of honey

1 teaspoon of salt

Turn the lamb in this fragrant bath at least five times. Place in an oven preheated to 450 degrees, still in the marinade, and baste frequently. Turn the leg of lamb lean side up for the first fifteen minutes; then turn the fat side up. Cook for an hour and forty-five minutes for pink meat, two hours and fifteen minutes for well-done meat. The marinade will·begin to crust on the surface.

JACQUES LIPCHITZ ⚄ LAMB CHOPS COOKED ON A GRAPEVINE I have to confess in the old times I used to be very interested in cooking...in the old times it would not have mattered to me if you said I was a bad sculptor. But a bad cook—I would not forgive you. This means that I could give you many recipes which would not be too different from what you can find in any good cookbook.

Let me tell you about some extraordinary meals which I had the opportunity to make in my life. Around 50 years ago, being very poor, I let myself be hired for the harvest of grapes in the region of Médoc in France. After a day of harvesting we would have our meals in the field. And I remember some very simple lamb chops grilled on the wood of the grapevine and that with Médoc wine. I can never forget the sumptuousness, the richness of this taste. Try it under the same condition, and I am sure I will hear from you.

161

PIERRE MONOSIET ♫ HAITIAN VOODOO BARBECUED GOAT While I was a young boy, whenever I was in the mountains for a few days, I loved to visit the peasants to see how they ate. Besides the plantain cooked right in the ashes, or the sweet potatoes broiled in cane sugar juice, my favorite dish will remain smoked, cured goat meat *(cabrit boucanné)*.

Let me remember one I ate years ago, made by an old servant of my family. She chose a young goat (the oldest are reserved for voodoo ceremonies and are called *dogoue*). It was killed that evening and seasoned early the following morning. The seasoning was hot and delicious: one or two pimientos, finely-chopped; a clove of garlic, several grains of black pepper and some cloves, the juice of a lemon and an orange. After three hours in this marinade she added a cup of water for the three pounds of meat and boiled it until tender. (She covered her iron pot with a few banana leaves for the best result.) Then she smoked the meat on the charcoals left from her wood fire, after having gently dropped it in some melted butter and lemon juice. During this time many tiny goats were grazing in the mountains and others were taking a nap in the shade.

For you, here is my own recipe:

162

Juice of one orange

Juice of one lime

1 teaspoon of Tabasco sauce

1 medium onion, grated

Whole pepper and cloves to taste

3 pounds of goat meat (or, if you like, I suggest lamb or deer;

my sister says why not young rhinoceros)

Pickle the meat in the marinade for 3 hours. Then add a cup of water and steam the meat until it is tender. Dip the meat in a sauce:

$\frac{1}{2}$ pound of melted butter

1 teaspoon of lime juice

$\frac{1}{2}$ teaspoon of salt

A few drops of garlic

And smoke over an open fire.

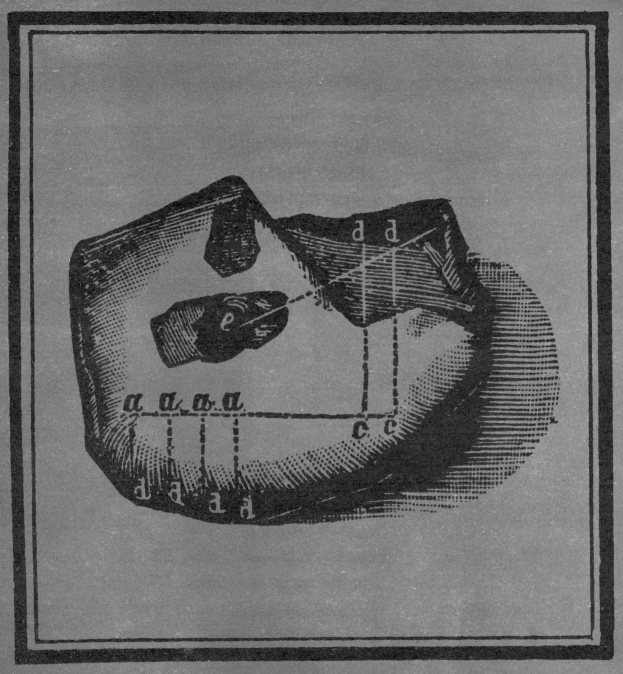

VEAL

165

GEORGES SIMENON ♌ FRICANDEAU A L'OSEILLE *Larded Meat with Sorrel*

It is sometimes difficult for me to make a distinction between taste and smell, between the pleasure of eating and the pleasure of sniffing an atmosphere.

When away from America, for example, I dream about the thick smell of eggs and bacon, with the more subtle coffee fragrance coming out of all quiet little places along the roads, even though my favorite American dish is clam chowder.

In London, haddock is my first choice for breakfast; in Holland, soft white bread with creamy cheese.

What about Paris? For me, as for my friend Maigret, the most genuine smell of the little bistros as well as that of the *loges de concierges,* the smell of old, narrow streets and of creaking staircases, is given by *le fricandeau a l'oseille.*

It's not always easy to find fresh sorrel in America (I used to plant some in my garden in Connecticut) but if you are lucky you can try this recipe, and for a few hours your home will have the aroma of a centuries-old house in Paris.

Take a fillet of veal and lard its surface with very fine lardons of pork. Place the meat in a stewing dish, add one or two diced carrots, onions, a bunch of parsley, bay leaves, thyme, one or two cloves, then half a cup of stock. Season with salt and pepper. Baste often while cooking so that the meat becomes a lovely golden colour.

After two and a half hours, the meat will be cooked. The gravy must then be transferred to a small saucepan and reduced slowly. Set the meat on a bed of sorrel, prepared as follows.

Take four or five handfuls of sorrel. Pare, cut away stalks, wash well. Then, place in a saucepan or casserole on low heat and reduce. When it is half reduced, add a tablespoonful of butter and cook until it is puréed. Pour gravy obtained from the veal (as above) over sorrel. Serves 4.

Fillet of veal, 1½ lbs.

Lardons of pork

2 diced carrots

Onions, 2 medium

A bunch of parsley

Bay leaves

Thyme

One or two cloves

Half a cup of stock

Salt, pepper

Sorrel

Butter

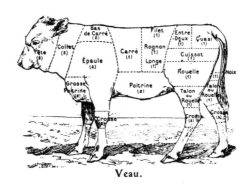

Veau.

JOHN LEVEE 🔊 **VEAU NORMAND** Sauté *slowly* in a covered pan the onions and mushrooms, with the thyme and bay leaf, in as little oil as possible. Remove the onions and mushrooms and the bay leaf and fry the veal in the resulting liquid, adding a little more oil if necessary. Fry the veal quickly until crisp. Remove the meat and return the vegetables to the pan. Add the sour cream and melted butter and stir gently over a low fire. Serve the meat, covered with sauce, with boiled or steamed rice or heated,

167

canned very small peas. The meat, cream and butter measurements are for a serving for four. The mushrooms, onions, and spices can be varied according to individual taste.

½ cup sliced fresh mushrooms

2 small onions, sliced or chopped

Thyme, bay leaf

1 pound veal, cut as for *scaloppini*

2 cups sour cream

2 tablespoons melted butter

2 cups cooked rice or

1 can small peas

Russian Sledge.

MICHEL LARIONOV ♫ VEAL A LA RUSSE

2 pounds of veal

Butter, melted

Four large onions, sliced

1 clove of garlic, chopped

Cut the two pounds of veal into bite-size cubes and brown them in the melted butter.

Slice the onions into the pan and add the chopped garlic. Cook them slowly until golden. Then add the following ingredients:

1 cup of bouillon

1 teaspoon of salt

$\frac{1}{2}$ teaspoon of freshly-ground pepper

1 teaspoon of paprika

1 teaspoon of grated nutmeg

1 tablespoon of sugar

$\frac{1}{2}$ teaspoon of mace

Simmer until the meat is tender, about $2\frac{1}{2}$ hours. Then add:

1 cup of sour cream

and cook another 15 to 20 minutes. Serve immediately with noodles *al dente*. Serves 4.

LOUIS AUCHINCLOSS ✍ VEAL BIRDS Have your butcher pound out, in squarish shape, veal *scaloppini* — reasonably large — two per person, and buy the same number of slices of boiled ham (you can always use the scraps), a bunch of parsley, a good, hard yellow cheese and three onions. Lay the *scaloppini* flat on a meat or bread board and place a piece of ham, of about the same size, on top. Put a piece of yellow cheese, about the size of a thumb, in the middle, then a sprig of parsley and a slice of onion, roll it all up and fasten it with string or, if you are lazy, with toothpicks, so that the stuffing is entirely enclosed. Fry lightly in butter in a heavy pan, browning all sides. Remove the birds.

Make a cream sauce using the juice in the pan and flour, cream, veal stock (or chicken consommé if you haven't got the former) and a good white wine or champagne.

Return the birds to the pan, cover tightly and simmer over a very low flame for $1\frac{1}{4}$

hours. They should be served with fluffy white rice, a good crisp mixed green salad and a dry white wine. Serves 6.

$1\frac{1}{2}$ lbs. veal *scaloppini* $\frac{1}{2}''$ thick

6 pieces boiled ham

Parsley

$\frac{1}{4}$ lb. yellow cheese

Three onions

Butter

Flour

Veal stock or chicken consommé

White wine or champagne

Cream

ANYA SETON ⑤ SWEETBREADS ANYA Blanch a pair of sweetbreads in the usual way, but I do it in canned or fresh chicken soup. (I cook almost everything in soup, especially vegetables.)

Make a white sauce with thin cream, sherry and onion juice. Carefully blend mayonnaise with it, as much as it will take without curdling. The sauce should be quite thick Flavor the sauce to taste with "Accent" and freshly-ground pepper. Bre breads into small pieces and cook them a moment in the sauce.

Split English muffins and toast them very lightly. Butter the halves and place upon each one a thin slice of ham. (I usually use Polish ham.)

Spoon the creamed sweetbreads lavishly over each muffin-and-ham half, in a mound which may be topped with a slice of truffle. Put the creations under the broiler and let them brown lightly. Serve at once. Four muffin halves are usually just enough to serve two people.

For those who like tarragon, that dried herb sprinkled into the white sauce adds a seductive flavor. Serves 2.

A pair of sweetbreads

Chicken soup, canned or fresh

Cream

2 tablespoons sherry

1 tablespoon onion juice

Mayonnaise

2 English muffins

4 thin slices of Polish ham

Several slices of truffle

Accent

Freshly-ground pepper

ENID FOSTER  BRAINS IN BEER Don't bother to parboil and skin the brains but rinse and drop into a heavy metal pot where whole green onions float in boiling sweet butter. Add ten kernels of whole black pepper. Stew until the brains are cooked. Pour in a bottle of Budweiser beer and recite three Hail Marys, then move brains to a serving dish. Add chopped parsley to liquid still on the stove and stir in enough flour to thicken almost to batter consistency. Spread over brains and add a generous garnish of grated lemon rind. One set of brains per person.

PORK

173

Sucking Pig.

KAREL APPEL 🐚 **COCHON BLOUSON NOIR A LA CREME (BEATNIK PIG WITH CREAM)** With a sharp knife make small openings and push cloves of garlic into the uncooked meat. Wrap the pig in fatty bacon and roast in a medium oven. About an hour before the meat is done surround it with washed, cored but unpeeled apples. Mix the white pepper, salt and a dash of curry with the whipped cream. When the pig is done, cover it with the seasoned whipped cream and serve.

A suckling pig

Apples

Fresh garlic cloves

White pepper, to taste

Whipped cream

Salt

Curry powder

Bacon for larding

CORNEILLE 🐚 **PORC A LA FRISONNE** (The Frisonne is the Hintelopen region of Holland.) In a heavy pan brown the cubed pork which has been lightly salted. Add the sliced onion and pepper, then the grated cabbage, *half* of the paprika and *half* of the sour cream. Cook over a low fire for one and a half or two hours. Fifteen minutes before it is done, add the rest of the paprika and immediately before serving, the remainder of the cream. Serve with rice or boiled potatoes. Serves 4 - 6.

1 pound of cubed pork

1 large onion, sliced

1 pepper, sliced

1 pound cabbage, grated

$\frac{1}{2}$ pint sour cream

2 or 3 teaspoons paprika

PEARL S. BUCK ⟨⟩ **SWEET-SOUR SPARERIBS** Cut ribs into separate pieces and cook in water with soy sauce and salt. Bring to a boil and turn down heat and let simmer for one hour. Transfer to frying pan, add remaining ingredients and fry until gravy becomes translucent. Serves 4.

$2\frac{1}{2}$ pounds spareribs

2 cups water

4 tablespoons soy sauce

1 teaspoon salt

3 tablespoons sugar, or honey

3 tablespoons vinegar

2 tablespoons cornstarch (optional)

$\frac{1}{2}$ cup water

2 tablespoons sherry, or brandy

1 teaspoon fresh, grated ginger root

Editors' note: Ginger root can be obtained in Chinese or Indian markets. When unavailable, ground ginger may be used.

PIERRE SOULAGES 🎝 LES IOLES *A Sausage Made from a Pig's Stomach* Soak the pig's stomach in water for several hours. Force coarsely-ground black pepper into the flesh by pounding it in with a flat, blunt object. (A pestle will do.) Force enough pepper into the skin until the meat is blackened. Cure the meat by hanging it to dry for 2 or 3 months. When cured, boil in water for 3 or 4 hours. Cut as desired and serve with potatoes. This recipe is from Rodez in the Dordogne region of France, region of the Lascaux caves. Serves 4.

Pig's stomach

Freshly-ground black pepper

Potatoes

Red River-hog (*Potamochœrus penicillatus*).

NORMAN KANTER 🎝 SAUSAGE A LA HARICOTS VERTS Fry: pork link sausage until lightly browned. Add: 1 package of frozen French cut green beans. Heat until beans are thawed and have begun to cook. Add: tomatoes, garlic, oregano, salt and pepper. Cook until the beans are tender. Serves 4.

1 package frozen French cut green beans

16 pork sausage links

To taste:

tomatoes, garlic, oregano,

salt and pepper

176

CALVIN KENTFIELD ℒ POT-AU-FEU DE POCAHONTAS This is an American Indian recipe that I made up — *I* am an American Indian — while living in London and watching the judo school across Gilston Road. I didn't really make it up, it's been in my family for generations, and it was originally intended to contain the head of an Englishman named John Smith — though it has since been supposed that any English head would have done. That it did not contain Smith's head is due, so family legend has it, to the cook, Pocahontas herself, who preferred to use the fellow whole. It was a meal eaten originally during certain tribal rites in October when the last goose had flown, and was, therefore, both secret and sacred. It was made available to the world, however, in the early nineteenth century by a renegade who pushed his way into the interior of Europe with the recipe sewn inconspicuously inside his scalp thus accounting for the obvious French corruptions. All these things considered, however, it's still very good.

Soak half a pound of butter beans, then put them in a big black iron pot. Remove the rind from half a pound of lean boiling bacon, and cut the meat into large chunks adding it to the beans together with a skinned onion stuck with a few cloves. Water to cover. No salt.

While the beans are boiling, mix in a large bowl — using your fingers so that everything will be evenly distributed — a pound of pork sausage, three medium onions roughly chopped, some mace, some thyme, and some ground black pepper. Brown this off in a heavy skillet until most of the fat is rendered out and the meat is cooked.

When the beans and bacon are tender, drain the water off but don't throw it away. Remove the clove-onion and dump the sausage mixture into the pot with the beans and bacon and add a large can (or a package of frozen) whole-kernel corn, a bay leaf, several peppercorns, and four or five ounces of tomato paste.

(When the Pilgrim fathers landed at Plymouth, Mass., they found tomato paste in wide use among my aboriginal ancestors — a phenomenon that has been fairly well explained in recent times by the discovery of the name Paolo Tortoni, the reckless younger son of a Neapolitan provisions house, among the newly-unearthed list of Columbus's officers. As for the canned corn, the Indians, of course, used it fresh off the cob.)

Add enough of the bean and bacon broth to make the pot moist enough to cook without burning and bubble a little. Cover and simmer over low gas for a long time until all the flavors are blended. Salt to taste after cooking. Serves one tribe.

½ lb. butter beans
½ lb. boiling bacon
Onion
Cloves
1 lb. pork sausage
3 chopped onions
Mace, thyme, ground black pepper
1 can corn, or 1 package frozen
Bay leaf, peppercorns
5 ounces tomato paste

CURRIES

179

DACHINE RAINER ✌ CURRY I always think of a man when I'm cooking, not of one man, but of one per recipe, and I think of him not in the ordinary sort of way; that is, not in order to meander that well-traveled channel between his heart and stomach. That impressed me as a route for a canal construction engineer and not for a cook — a helpless, female cook. It seems quixotic to fix oneself in a man's heart when one can secure him eternally in one's memory.

Every man is not an exceptional cook but every man I've come to know...well... has, in his book of tricks, at least one remarkable recipe. It is a slow process to cull this forth. Men seem content to permit their ladies, night after night, to wrestle with dinner when it is manifestly apparent — invariably to themselves, and most generally as a conversational gambit — that they could improve matters considerably. Consequently, it takes me a number of years to acquire a man's most splendid culinary performance by heart and by that time, not infrequently, I'm no longer interested in cooking it for him.

Thus I learned a superb spaghetti sauce from wandering around with an Italian street musician; lamb, red cabbage and string beans from a Greek philosopher, and a magnificent clam chowder from settling down, briefly, with a clam digger on Long Island.

Through my association with Mohib A———, a Mohammedan, a native of Assam province, India, I acquired (along with a stint in the Woman's Home of Detention on the not-too-preposterous charge of possessing illegal firearms) my most formidable recipe. Curry.

To make a great curry you have to establish a Zen kind of concentration. It will not do to work out your latest *Sturm und Drang* or think up a zany plot for a novel while preparing a curry. That requires altogether another sort of dish.[1]

Nevertheless, curry is not an exotic dish. It is not for a rare occasion. For optimum appreciation, it should be prepared night after night for weeks, for months, years at a time until one becomes an addict and will eat nothing else. Curry for two:

1 pound of beef, cut small, or

1 pound of lamb, or

1 pound of fish fillet (cod is exceptionally good, or

8 hard-cooked eggs, halved, or

A brace of pigeons cut in pieces, or

1 pound of dried split peas

1 pound of rice (if Oriental), or

$\frac{1}{2}$ pound of rice (if Occidental)

1 pound of onions

5 cloves of garlic

5 bay leaves

7 whole cloves

3 sticks of cinnamon

3 tablespoons of curry powder

1 lemon, sliced lengthwise

A pigeon-egg-sized lump of butter

Now for the cooking. The tempo is important. The first stage must be as swift as possible:

Toss a quantity of cow butter or vegetable oil into a heavy iron cauldron, in the meantime groaning melodramatically that you're fresh out of water buffalo or yak butter.[2]

Throw in the thinly-sliced onions, the quantity to be determined, in exact ratio, pound for pound, by the quantity of meat, fowl,[3] fish, eggs or dried peas. Stir for a moment, then add meat and garlic and continue stirring — above the fiercest heat possible — until the onions disintegrate entirely, forming a thick sauce. Cover ingredients with water and bring to a boil, then turn down to simmer; add bay leaves, cloves, cinnamon and a reliable curry powder.[4]

Simmer approximately an hour for meat or peas, half for fowl and no more than five minutes for fish or cooked eggs. Any of these curries will profit by being made in the morning or the night before; the sauce will ingratiate itself into the primary substance. Reheat.

The curry should be accompanied by rice. And, for goodness' sake, don't goof the dinner by not having the rice perfect. You should be able to prepare rice by now. If you can't, find out how elsewhere or skip the whole thing.

With the rice and curry serve a good, homemade chutney. Do not clutter the dining table with a maze of condiments: peanuts, pickled beets, olives, mustard pickles...this is not a *smörgåsbord*. Serve a side dish of only chutney.

The primary ingredient is, of course, the mango, but peaches will do. Do not consider either canned, yet, in the event that you suddenly acquire a gift of a bushel of mangoes or peaches, you may make up a quantity of chutney and can it yourself. The ingredients may fluctuate and if it resembles a good, sweet piccalilli, you will have done very well:

1 apple

5 mangoes or peaches

$\frac{1}{3}$ pound of raisins

182

1 sweet onion

3 green tomatoes

Sugar (white or brown)

Cider

7 cloves

Nutmeg, cinnamon and, optionally, angostura

Chop coarsely the apple, mangoes, onion and tomatoes; combine and cover with sugar and cider; add cloves, a dash of nutmeg, 3 dashes of angostura (optional and quixotic) and the veriest sprinkle of cinnamon.

Remember the slices of lemon. These you may squirt on the curry, suck on during the frequent intermissions necessary to cool your burning mouth, and rub between your fingers as a method of rinsing your hand. Do this at intervals or at the end of the meal, but not before you have sucked most of the sauce off first; off the fingers of your right hand or your left, as the case may be.[5]

Do you want dessert after this? Mangoes. Nothing else will do.

Now you may have tea and chew betel nuts. Do not serve tea with dinner and certainly — this is Mohammedan cookery — no alcohol.[6] Have a water pitcher. You'll need it.

A curry dinner, provided you overeat the proper amount, makes you indolent and sensual.[7] Don't plan on doing anything strenuous afterwards — that is, not too strenuous.[8]

By way of postscript and a warning. Leftover curry: do not make sandwiches of it the next day.

---

[1] *For example, I make a psychologically-troubled soup. In it I ferociously pick and slice and chop up anything I find in the garden or the larder — vegetables and herbs and bits of flowers — and after the bones and onions brown and it all begins to boil and bubble, it occurs to me that I'm stewing impertinent editors in my cauldron and wayward children and miscreant husbands. However, a curry is indifferent to your literary and personal problems.*

[2] *This is the traditional ingredient; however, in its absence, goat butter is the best substitute.*

[3] *Pigeon is more properly game than fowl. To secure them according to proper ritual, you probably have to be living in Norfolk Street on New York's lower East Side and so much in love that you're willing to go up on the roof and steal them from your neighbor's roost and wring their necks. (If you want to buy a chicken, instead, go ahead.)*

[4] *The house will reek — a delirious kind of aromatics — of curry for days. I have an imaginative friend who claims that having succumbed to its heavy aroma all one winter (he and a colleague were starting the Grove Press in his living room on Grove Street) as I alternated between addressing envelopes, drinking Alexanders and cooking, that he now smells it in absolute conjunction with me, everywhere, always in Grove Street and even in the resinous pine woods through which he walks whenever he visits me in my log cabin.*

[5] *Two centuries after its invention, the fork still has a limited utility and none at all for curry. To get the most sensual pleasure out of curry, you must be a mimic — and historically accurate. Use the first four fingers, slightly cupped, of your dominant hand, as a small derrick — to scoop up first a bit of rice then a bit of curry and then direct your thumb as a shovel to maneuver the delectables (all of it, now!) into your mouth. Sit on your minor or inactive hand so you're not tempted to use both hands. After you dig the procedure, you may use your non-eating hand to gesture with. It looks elegant to eat with one hand, particularly if you're seated cross-legged on a pillow on the floor.*

[6] *I know no better — that is, I know no other — reason for giving up lush, temporarily or permanently. On the other hand, I do question whether it's desirable to tangle with Indian men at all, curry notwithstanding. They can cook and . . . and . . . but, absurdly romantic, they are aware of their national heritage far beyond the call of simple chauvinism. Each male relives his glorious past in some reincarnation of Akbar in a way in which it would never occur to a poor Greek hashing potatoes in some diner whose past, when one considers it, is fairly glorious too. Indians — they're impetuous, passionate and violent. That's the way a good curry is.*

[7] *If you overeat the improper amount, it acts as a soporific.*

[8] *See Ajanta cave drawings for the most on that subject.*

Java Hen.

KRISHNA REDDY ꕥ CURRIED CHICKEN WITH YOGHURT CHUTNEY

Cut the chicken into serving pieces, smear them with the turmeric powder. Place in a kettle. Cover with water, add salt, cover and simmer until tender. Remove the chicken and save the broth.

Heat half the butter in a large frying pan, add garlic, onion, curry powder, corian-

184

der, cloves and cinnamon. Cook, stirring until the onion is golden brown. Add the remaining butter and the chicken. Cook the chicken until brown, about 20 minutes. Mix the flour with the broth in which the chicken was stewed and add it to the frying chicken. Add slices of tomato if desired. Cover and cook one half hour until the sauce is cooked down. Arrange on a warm platter and surround with hot saffron rice. Serves 6.

Coriander (*Coriandrum sativum*).

1 roasting chicken

1 sliced onion

2 cloves chopped garlic

2 tablespoons curry powder

2 tablespoons flour

6 cups hot saffron rice

1 tablespoon coriander

$\frac{1}{2}$ teaspoon turmeric

5 cloves

2 sticks cinnamon

5 tablespoons butter

Salt to taste

Yoghurt Chutney: Add to the yoghurt the onions, salt, white raisins, ground coconut and small pieces of tomato. Mix well. Sprinkle a teaspoon of lemon juice over the mixture and serve with curried chicken and saffron rice.

1 pint yoghurt

½ cup ground coconut

½ cup raisins (white)

1 teaspoon lemon juice

2 tomatoes, cut in pieces

2 onions, finely-chopped

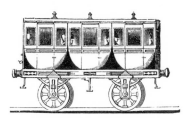

ANTHONY POWELL ℌ FARMHOUSE CURRY I have never been to India. My great-grandfather was an officer in the Honourable East India Company's Naval Service and two of his brothers were in the Company's armies of Madras and Bombay. That cannot be called a close connection; but I can never remember a time, however young, when I did not like curry. For many years I have frequented Indian restaurants in London, even eating, sometimes with enjoyment, that dish served on the luncheon cars of British Railways, paradoxically named on the menu: *Farmhouse Curry*.

In order to be self-supporting, so far as curry is concerned, I learned to cook it for myself. I find that the following method takes not less than an hour and a half; two hours to be free from all pressure of time.

Take three onions of medium size and chop them coarsely. Some people add two cloves of garlic, but I do not think that essential. If you use the garlic, chop it fine. Put these to cook gently in three tablespoonfuls of olive oil. They can be cooked until soft and not brown, but if allowed to brown (and I see no objection) the curry is a darker, richer colour. Add a tablespoonful of flour and stir in. Add two tablespoonfuls of curry powder. The amount of curry powder you use varies to some extent with the heat of the curry; and, of course, your own and your guests' taste. Cook very gently seeing that the onions do not stick to the pan. Add an apple, peeled, cored and cut into thin slices. The longer you can cook at this stage, the better. The flavour steadily improves. Add three tomatoes, peeled, and chopped coarsely with all their juice. Add some stock (of which you will need a pint) and let the curry bubble and hiss. At first, a pint of stock may seem too much, but as the curry cooks, the stock will be absorbed. Again, it is a question of taste how liquid you like your curry to be. Add a teaspoon of salt, a teaspoon of sugar, cinnamon and nutmeg, with other mixed spices, a tablespoon of coconut, a handful of raisins, a tablespoon of mango chutney (or other chutneys, to taste), a squeeze of lemon juice, and more stock. This can simmer all day, if that suits you, or can be allowed to cool and be warmed up some days later when it will have improved. If you let it cool, the curry should be taken from the pan and put in a dish. Half an hour before you propose to eat the curry, put the meat in — say one pound of lean cooked meat. Pork is always good, or chopped-up sausages of all kinds. It must have the fat removed. If you use uncooked meat, it must be cooked with the onion and curry powder. People are naturally inclined to use leftover meats for curry, and if really good meat is used, the result is correspondingly good. Serve with boiled rice (kept separate from the curry), Bombay duck (a kind of dried fish), popadams (thin, circular, biscuit-like objects) —

187

both dried previously in the oven — and chutney. Fried bananas (one per person at least) are also very good as they relieve the palate from the heat of the curry. The curry powder can be mixed with vinegar which gives the curry a rather sharper, but less "hot" taste. Shrimps, prawns or eggs can be used instead of meat. If eggs are used, they should be hard-boiled, cut in half, and set on the curry. Odds and ends of vegetables greatly improve a curry. Potato can be used, chopped up, in moderation.

Allow a cup of rice per head. Fill a large saucepan three-quarters full with water, add a tablespoon of salt and bring to the boil. When it is boiling hard, put in the rice gradually so that the water remains boiling, and keep it there for 12 minutes, removing the scum with a spoon. The time of boiling can be varied by testing the rice with the teeth. Rices vary somewhat. When the rice is soft, but firm, remove the saucepan from the fire, turn into a colander, and hold under the cold tap. This separates the grains of rice. You should previously have warmed a dish into which some melted butter has been placed. Pour the rice, from which the water has now been drained, into the dish, mixing it with the butter with a fork. The rice should preferably be put in a fireproof dish which is then put under the grill for a minute or two before serving.

Curry is a delightful change from almost every form of everyday cooking. It is admirable in hot weather — for which it is, of course, designed — and good for a hangover. It is the perfect medium for bringing together East and West. The remains can later be used for mulligatawny soup. Curry for ten:

Three medium-sized onions, coarsely chopped
Two cloves of garlic, chopped fine (optional)
Three tablespoonfuls of olive oil
One tablespoonful of flour
Two tablespoonfuls of curry powder (variable)
An apple, peeled, cut into thin slices
Three tomatoes, peeled and chopped

A pint of stock (variable)

A teaspoon of salt

A teaspoon of sugar

A teaspoon of cinnamon, nutmeg and other mixed spices

A tablespoon of coconut

A handful of raisins

A tablespoon of mango chutney (or other chutneys)

Flowering Branch of Mango-tree (*Mangifera Indica*).

A squeeze of lemon juice

One pound of meat, or shrimps or eggs

Boiled rice

Vinegar (optional to make the curry less "hot")

Odds and ends of vegetables (if you have them)

Potato (if you wish)

Bombay duck

Popadams

Fried bananas

HAROLD COUSINS ⌘ INDONESIAN RICE TABLE This is a most flexible dish and the variations are as many as the cook can concoct. Basically the meal begins with a dish of light, fluffy rice and a curry sauce. *Curry Sauce:* Season two cups of meat stock with salt, pepper and curry powder to taste. Heat. Mix one tablespoon of cornstarch with one cup of cold milk until the cornstarch is smoothly blended, then add this mixture gradually to the boiling meat stock. Slice raw mushrooms and add to the sauce. Serve in separate dishes, the following — ⌘ *Meat Dish:* Fry a mixture of diced beef steak, veal cutlet and pork tenderloin in butter. Season with salt, pepper, nutmeg, Indian sambals, sugar and diced onions. Serve hot. ⌘ *Shrimp:* Lightly fry small shrimp with onion and sliced celery stalk. Add molasses. Serve hot. ⌘ *Egg Plant:* Fry egg plant and tomato, add sugar, salt, Indian sambals, raisins and nutmeg. Serve hot. ⌘ *String Bean Salad:* Serve finely-cut cold cooked string beans, mixed with raw onion, peanut oil, and lemon juice to taste. Salt and pepper. Serve chilled. ⌘ *Celery Root:* Dice celery root and onion. Fry in butter. Season with salt and cinnamon. A few slices of sausage may be added if desired. ⌘ *Fried Banana:* Fry in butter four or five bananas until soft and light brown. Mash. Add blanched almonds, cinnamon. Serve hot. For 6.

Banana (*Musa sapientum*).

LOUIS AUCHINCLOSS ᔓ A NOTE ON CURRY I wonder if I really believe in food as a means of ethnic communication. I always think of taste as subjective, hence universal. It should have no national confines. I will not admit, for example, to a good *Indian* curry. It is a good curry. The way of making it is not Indian; it is the only way. I remember a UN delegate from an Eastern nation who tried to raise a laugh at a dinner party in New York at the expense of America, by describing how we make iced coffee: "First boil the water, then pour it on ice." He was answered with the shout of protest, "Cuisine!" He did not understand until it was drubbed into his thick head that such was not the *American* way of making iced coffee. It was the *only* way. Perhaps the principle of cuisine may be the ultimate principle of world peace.

Editors' note: In a letter to Mr. Auchincloss, the editors suggested that food is a means of "ethnic communication."

191

PALME D'HONNEUR

HORS CONCOURS

ROUEN   1885

A FEW SAUCES

193

LYNN CHADWICK ❧ GARLIC MAYONNAISE (AIOULI) Add salt and pepper to the yolk of one egg and stir well. Gradually add, drop by drop, about ¾ of a cup of olive oil. After the mayonnaise has begun to stiffen, in between drops of olive oil add, equally gradually, garlic juice to taste — about two tablespoons. Remember to stir constantly. Serve with any simply-prepared fish, cold chicken or cold meat.

NATALIA DUMITRESCO ❧ MOUSSE D'AIL *Garlic Sauce* Peel and mash several cloves of garlic in a wooden mortar. When the garlic is thoroughly mashed, add warm water and salt.

CESAR ❧ SPAGHETTI ROSINE (with fresh basil) Use freshly-made spaghetti in preference to packaged spaghetti, which has a tendency to be doughy. Fresh spaghetti may be purchased in many Italian delicatessens. Also, use only fresh basil.

In a mortar place 4 cloves of garlic and crush them thoroughly. Then take a handful of fresh basil, broken into small pieces, and crush that. Add olive oil to the crushed

194

garlic and basil, mixing constantly, until the mixture is the consistency of mayonnaise. A little goat's cheese, of the most dry variety (*chèvre*) may be added if desired. Finally add half of a fresh, skinned tomato and continue to mix and crush until the sauce is smooth. Add olive oil as necessary.

Cook the spaghetti, drain it and spoon the sauce over the hot spaghetti. It will blend with it like butter. Serves 6.

Freshly-made spaghetti

4 cloves of garlic

A handful of fresh basil

Goat's cheese (*chèvre*) if desired

$\frac{1}{2}$ of a fresh, skinned tomato

Olive oil as needed

JAMES JONES 🦁 CHILI FROM MY BACHELOR DAYS This chili is best made by bachelors for their own consumption.

Fry onions in butter in a large, heavy pot. Then saute the hamburger meat. Turn down the flame or burner and pour in a medium-sized can of tomato juice. Toss in some whole, ripe tomatoes and add chili powder to taste, as much as you can stand. Lastly add two cans of kidney beans and let the chili cook for at least an hour. Serves one very hungry bachelor.

Onions, sliced or chopped

2 pounds of hamburger or ground round steak

1 can tomato juice, medium-sized

Several whole, ripe tomatoes

2 cans of kidney beans

Chili powder to taste

BURL IVES 🎵 BARBECUE SAUCE Stir all ingredients with a bindle stick. Add rosemary and thyme, a partridge and a pear tree. Serve over marinated beef. Prepare a bindle stick on the end of which make a sack. Fill the sack with fresh salt and pepper, rosemary and thyme. Dip into the sauce until the bag shrinks.

Wild, black honey

Turkish coffee, very thick

7 smashed garlic cloves

1 jigger of sake

1 jigger Danish cherry wine

Salt and pepper to taste

(5 jiggers spiced wine vinegar)

(7 cloves boiled in chicken blood)

FRANKLIN WATKINS 🎵 ALTERNATE TO WELSH RAREBIT This should be cooked and served hot in a glazed, open ovenproof crock. The crock should be high rather than flat and shallow. Ours happens to be cylindrical — about ten inches high and five inches in diameter.

6 slices Pepperidge Farm white bread,

buttered and cut into fingers

$1\frac{1}{4}$ lbs. mixed domestic cheeses cut into bits (sharp

Cheddar, Wisconsin Swiss, jack, etc.

Never use processed cheese)

Parmesan cheese, grated

4 whole eggs

2 cups milk

½ teaspoon salt

Pepper

Mouse (*Mus musculus*).

Butter the earthenware dish. Line the bottom and sides with bread. Put in half the mixed domestic cheeses, then layer of bread. Add remaining cheese. Beat eggs, add milk, salt and pepper. Pour this over the cheese and bread. Parmesan cheese should be added throughout and more sprinkled liberally over the top. Bake in a moderate oven 35 to 40 minutes. Serves 6.

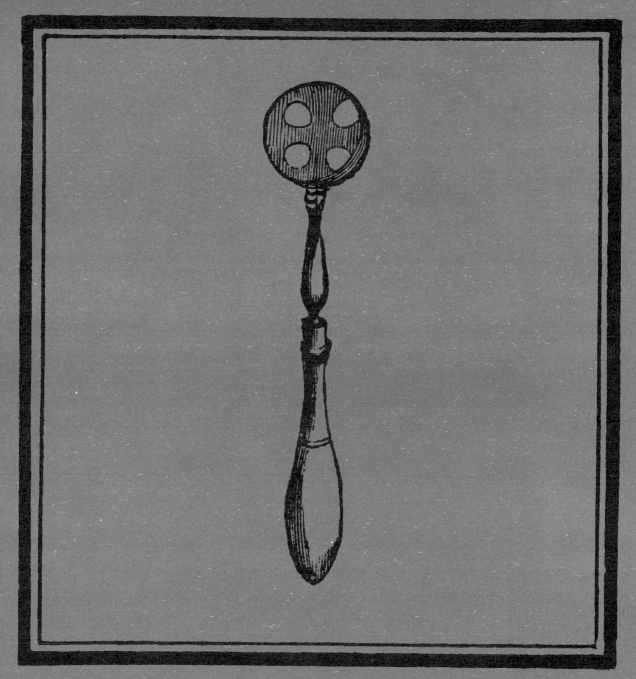

POTATOES, EGGPLANT

199

O vast earth-apple, waiting to be fried,
Of all life's starers the most many-eyed,
What furtive purpose hatched you long ago
In Indiana or in Idaho?

In Indiana and in Idaho
Snug underground, the great potatoes grow,
Puffed up with secret paranoias unguessed
By all the duped and starch-fed Middle West.

Like coiled-up springs or like a will-to-power,
The fat and earthy lurkers bide their hour,
The silent watchers of our raucous show
In Indiana or in Idaho.

"They deem us dull, a food and not a flower.
Wait! We'll outshine all roses in our hour.
Not wholesomeness but mania swells us so
In Indiana and in Idaho.

"In each Kiwanis Club on every plate,
So Bland and health-exuding do we wait
That Indiana never, never knows
How much we envy stars and hate the rose."

Some doom will strike (as all potatoes know)
When — once too often mashed in Idaho —
From its cocoon the drabbest of earth's powers
Rises and is a star.
And shines.
And lours.

This deliberately prosaic recipe I use for potatoes, plus my poem "To a Sinister Potato," illustrate how the prosaic becomes both sinister and poetic.

POTATOES ANNA

Use four average-sized raw potatoes, a quarter pound of butter, and paprika, pepper, salt. Pare the potatoes, cutting them into slices of *ca.* one-eighth inch. After plunking them in cold water, drain and dry. Spread melted butter over each slice; spread butter over a skillet; then place the slices into the skillet in three overlapping layers. Be lavish with paprika, moderate with salt and pepper; add butter to taste; keep for ten minutes in the oven at 450 degrees. After ten minutes, lower the heat and bake till brown in color, checking from time to time to avoid leaving them there too long. Reverse the skillet, upside-down, onto a platter before serving, so that you eat the bottom potatoes first. Serves 4.

4 medium raw potatoes

$\frac{1}{4}$ lb. butter

Paprika, salt, pepper

Butter, melted

Rotate Corolla of Potato
(*Solanum tuberosum* .

JOHN SACCARO  TIELA (*pronounced tee ella*) Butter an earthenware casserole. Slice the zucchini in ⅛ inch slices. Peel and slice potatoes. Chop parsley and garlic to a fine paste. Place in layers of zucchini in bottom of casserole, sprinkle cheese, bread crumbs, parsley and garlic over it. Dot with butter.

Place a layer of sliced potatoes over this, add cheese, bread crumbs and garlic, pour a few drops of olive oil over this.

Alternate with layers of zucchini, then potatoes with sprinkling of bread crumbs, cheese, parsley and garlic mixture until casserole is filled.

Top with crumb and cheese mixture, dot with butter. Add three tablespoons of water and cover. Place in 350 degree oven for one hour. Serves four.

3 potatoes

4 zucchini

1 cup bread crumbs

1 cup grated dry Monterey cheese

1 handful chopped parsley

2 cloves garlic

Salt and freshly-ground pepper, to taste

Olive oil

Butter

HARVEY SWADOS 🦁 **LATKES** *Potato Pancakes* This recipe is for those occasions when something different is required, when there is nothing in the house, or when the wife revolts and declines to cook.

Take 10 large potatoes, peel, then grate into bowl on fine side of the grater. If you use a blender, cut the potatoes in quarters first — but the texture of this finished *latke* will be somewhat different from that of the hand-rubbed one, and to my taste not quite so good. Grate or blend 2 medium-sized onions. Add 1 tablespoon of salt and some freshly-ground pepper. Stir until well blended.

Drop by large tablespoon into a frying pan with hot oil. The thinner you spread the batter, the crisper and tastier the *latkes*. Fry until golden brown on each side.

Serve with applesauce and a pitcher of cold milk. Hot tea may be substituted in winter. For some reason, *latkes* do not taste good with coffee. Makes about 30 *latkes*.

10 large potatoes

2 medium-size onions

2 eggs

½ cup of flour

1 tablespoon of salt

Freshly-ground pepper

Oil

DOUGLAS MOORE ℑ **CREAMED POTATOES** When you are making baked potatoes, put four or five aside to be used the next day. Cut them up in small pieces not larger than lima beans. Put them in an iron frying pan and season with salt, pepper, and dabs of butter. Then cover them with milk and cook slowly until they are well thickened. Add more milk and allow them to thicken again. The whole process should take about two hours. Be careful not to burn. Use no flour, for the thickening comes out of the potatoes themselves. All the milk must be absorbed for best results.

ARNOLD SINGER ℑ EGGPLANT CASSEROLE

PEEL AND CUBE:

1 eggplant

FRY:

chopped or sliced onions
chopped garlic and the cubed eggplant.

ADD:

oregano to taste
a little water and cover and steam.

COOK:

a box of egg noodles

ADD:

a large container of cottage or pot cheese
fold in eggplant mixture

put into a casserole
cover with:
sliced tomatoes
sliced Cheddar cheese
sliced ripe, black olives
BAKE UNTIL THE CHEESE MELTS.
Serves 4.

Flowering Branch and Fruit of Egg-plant
(*Solanum Melongena*).

ꙮ RICHARD EMIL BRAUN ꙮ
THREE GOOD THINGS TO DO WITH EGGPLANT

I

Something to smear on a salad of, say, endive, lettuce leaves, black-radish flakes, scallions, and sliced tomatoes, is prepared as follows: Bake an eggplant whole, turning it until it turns grease-black in spots and is turgid. Puncture it. (If it expires with a hiss and sags, it is well done. It may be flayed with ease.) Macerate. Refrigerate. Meanwhile, dice onions, nearly a third the bulk of eggplant, and drench with lemon juice. Mix with the eggplant.

Ingredients for salad (endive, scallions, etc.)

Baked eggplant, refrigerated after baking

Diced onions ($\frac{1}{3}$ the bulk of eggplant)

Lemon juice

II

To fix the best chicken I know, stuff with chunks of raw eggplant, quarters of onion, tomatoes, green peppers, and several cloves of garlic. Rub the fowl with olive oil and place in a glass bowl heaped with further eggplant and peppers, and cover with glass or foil. Bake slowly. Uncover to brown.

Chicken

Raw eggplant

Quarters of onion, tomatoes, green pepper

Several cloves of garlic

Olive oil

III

For meatballs, grind beef three times. Whiten one side of the mash with white pepper, and knead this in with grated garlic; surround with equal parts of eggplant, onions, and tomatoes in total mass equal to that of meat. Add a teaspoon of olive oil for every eight lumps. Bake covered until the onions are soggy, then leave exposed until half the juice evaporates.

Meatball meat

White pepper

Grated garlic

Eggplant

Olive oil, onion, tomatoes

PEAS AND BEANS

207

JACKSON BURGESS ⚬ HOPPIN' JOHN I know for a fact that Hoppin' John is eaten: I have seen the thing done. In fact, I eat it myself a couple of times a year. The real question is whether or not anybody actually *likes* Hoppin' John. I've asked myself if my own taste for it isn't really sentimentality or Southern chauvinism or that benign Deep South affectation called "acting *country*," but I always wind up answering that I like Hoppin' John.

Even in the deepest South, Hoppin' John isn't heard of much any more. It was always regarded by Southerners as poor folks' food, and transplanted Yankees don't seem to take to field peas as easily as they do to barbecue and corn bread. I don't know how it got its name (in some parts of the South it's simply called "peas and rice") and the *Dictionary of Americanisms* offers no help. *Americanisms* does contain the only recipes for Hoppin' John that I've ever seen in print, but they are marred by malice and envy, both examples being quoted from Yankee writers. Frederick Law Olmsted, writing in 1856 of his travels in the "Slave States," referred to "...the only luxury with which they are acquainted...a stew of bacon and peas with red pepper," and a *Chicago Daily News* story of 1948 is cited thus: "...Hopping John...seems to be compounded of cowpeas and melted horses' hoofs." The first is an open slander, and the second recipe is instantly discredited by its tone of levity and the fact that the poor fellow can't even spell "hoppin'."

Here's how I make it:

Wash half a pound of black-eyed peas and leave them in a large bowl to soak for six or eight hours in plenty of water. Pour off the water that's left after the peas soak, and add fresh water, very slightly salted, to boil them in. You need a big pot. When the peas

208

have boiled slowly for half an hour, add a quarter of a pound of fat back cut in chunks. Half an hour later, slice two medium-sized white onions into the pot. After another quarter of an hour, add a heaping handful of rice and red pepper to taste. If the peas have boiled down pretty thoroughly it may be necessary to add some water just before you put in the rice, since there has to be enough liquid for the rice to absorb. This is a matter of judgment. When the rice is done, the Hoppin' John is ready. Eat it hot. Half a pound of peas will make enough to serve four or five people. Stir Hoppin' John from time to time throughout its cooking, but don't worry about the scum that forms at first —it will disappear.

If you want to get some inkling of what reduced Jeeter Lester to depravity, serve your Hoppin' John with boiled turnip greens and a fried pone made of meal and water and salt, and eat this with the thought that tomorrow is Monday and back to lean rations. Serves 4.

½ pound black-eyed peas
¼ pound fat back
2 medium white onions
Handful of rice
Red pepper

MICHEL MISHORIT  HUMUS CHICK-PEAS (GARBANZOS) Take one cup raw chick-peas, soak overnight, then boil until well cooked. Cool off and smash thoroughly in a deep dish. Add some Sesame Tahina as already prepared.* Place it in a flat dish for serving, adding garlic, olive oil and chopped parsley on top. This should be eaten with a flat bread called Pittah. If you haven't Pittah, feed on bread, if you haven't bread, feed on cake. Serves 4.

*See Appetizers: Basic Sesame Tahina.

209

1 cup raw chick-peas

Sesame Tahina

Garlic

Olive oil

Chopped parsley

1. Branch of the Olive (*Olea Europæa*), with fruits.   2. Branch with
flowers.   *a*, a flower.

MUDITE AUSTRINA 𝔖 KAMI *Mythical Dish from the Latvian Past* Cook peas
till tender. Bake potatoes. Grind together. Fry onions with bacon in a skillet. Do not
remove the grease. Mix thoroughly with peas and potatoes, while hot. Mould in grenade-
like round balls. Serve cold or hot with churned milk for "fiestas." Feeds the multitude.

Several pounds of grey, large peas (imported from Canada or Europe)

Potatoes—a few

Bacon—a lot

Onions

Salt

210

RICHARD EMIL BRAUN ♫ A BETTER FORMULA FOR LENTILS Instead of introducing a ham bone and boiling to porridge, I do this:

While the lentils are frisking, still intact but soft, drain half the soup, sour the rest with cider vinegar, simmer a minute, then drip carmelized white sugar in and stir well. Serve, not as a soup, but as a sweet-and-sour side dish beside beef. (1 cup dried lentils yields 2 cups cooked, or 4 servings.)

Lentils

Cider vinegar

White sugar, carmelized

CHARLES ANGOFF ♫ LIMA BEAN TSIMESS Soak beans overnight in 3 quarts cold water. Discard any water not absorbed by beans before cooking. Combine water and soup cubes (or soup stock) with onions, bay leaf, celery, and oregano and bring to a boil. Add soaked lima beans and cook until almost dry.

Make a mixture of molasses, chili sauce, mustard, coffee and maple syrup. Grease slightly a 2 quart casserole and place in it a layer of cooked lima beans. Cover with slices of knockwurst and some of the molasses mixture. Repeat until all the beans have been used up, leaving some of the molasses mixture to cover the top layer of beans. Bake uncovered at 325° for 1 hour. Serves 6 - 8.

2 cups dried lima beans

1 quart boiling water with

2 large chicken cubes (or, 1 quart soup stock)

1 small onion

1 bay leaf

1 large stalk celery with leaves

1 sprig parsley

Dash of oregano

½ cup unsulphured molasses

¼ cup chili sauce

3 tablespoons prepared mustard

¼ cup maple syrup or dark brown sugar

2 tablespoons very strong coffee

2 knockwursts, sliced in rings

Variation: Instead of knockwurst rings, canned pineapple chunks may be used.

Comment: In our family, generation after generation has known that if this dish is prepared with loving care, those eating it for 100 years are assured a long life.

LES TOMATES.

JOHN LEVEE ⌘ HARICOTS VERTS AUX TOMATES Cook the ingredients slowly in a covered casserole until the beans are done but still crisp. A generous amount of garlic is recommended and sliced fresh green pepper may be added for variation. And/or sliced sweet onion. Serve as a vegetable, hot or chilled, with veal or chicken. Serves 4.

1 pound fresh string beans
1 pound tomatoes
Garlic
Olive oil
Salt and pepper to taste
Thyme
Bay leaf
Cayenne powder to taste

LEAVES AND A LILY

215

RICHARD EMIL BRAUN ℌ A HAPPY STARCH AND VEGETABLE Snap egg noodles into quarter-inch squares. Boil. Rinse rapidly with cold water. Drain.

Slice the same amount of green cabbage into cubes the same size. Steam this till tender. Drain.

Mix noodles and cabbage in a pot. Bake open, with a quarter-pound of butter per quart of mixture. Turn each time the surface browns, until crisp cubes are visible throughout.

This should be well salted.

Drink beer.

Egg noodles

Green cabbage

Quarter-pound of butter per quart of mixture

I have really no need of adding, but I shall add that no dish is worth preparing unless it is prepared for the sake either of love, or of conviviality, or of a loftily-hermitical renunciation of both. Otherwise, it is better to think of nourishment. (The same test may be applied to any physical exercise or cultural pursuit.)

KENNETH PATCHEN ℌ CABBAGE CROQUETTES FINNISH STYLE *A Recipe of One of the Great Cooks, My Mother-in-law, Olga Florrell.* Parboil good-size head of cabbage. Separate leaves and drain excess moisture. Put through medium grinder. Make cup of white sauce with equal parts canned milk and cabbage liquid, add

to cabbage. Beat 3 eggs and add to mixture. Now put in enough bread crumbs so that little hats may be formed. Fry in deep fat until crisply brown. Particularly delicious with pork roasted with soy and almond (or raisin) seasoning. Serves 6.

1 good-size head of cabbage

Evaporated milk

3 eggs

Bread crumbs

RICHARD WILBUR   TWO CHARD DISHES   Swiss chard is a plant of the beet family which out-regenerates everything else in the garden, and any plant so responsive to our hunger ought not to be wasted. Here is a recipe, southern French in origin, which uses both the stalks and the leaves and produces two chard dishes for the same meal.

Dish I: Remove from the stalks enough leaves to fill a large kettle. Boil for two minutes in the water left on the leaves from the washing. Chop, and add one minced onion, one half stick of butter, two teaspoonfuls of *fines herbes,* the juice of half a lemon, and salt and pepper to taste. Turn over in a buttered skillet until the onion is soft.

Swiss chard (leaves)

1 onion

2 ounces butter

2 teaspoons *fines herbes*

Juice of half a lemon

Salt and pepper to taste

Dish II: Take perhaps twelve large stalks and cut them into three-inch lengths. Then make a suitable quantity of ordinary pancake batter, adding two eggs and a teaspoonful of baking powder. Dip the salted stalks in the batter and fry in two cups of Crisco until golden brown and puffy. Salt lightly, and place in warm oven until served. Serves four to six people.

Swiss chard (12 stalks)

Pancake batter

2 eggs

1 teaspoon baking powder

2 cups Crisco

My only contribution to cookery, I am afraid, is the technical word "purse." *Crêpes* are ready to be turned when they "purse."

FELIX RUVULO 🎵 **BROCCOLI AFUCATO** *Smothered Sicilian Broccoli* Pare away the hard cores of two bunches of fresh broccoli. Split the stalks and place, flower out, like a wheel, in a flat, round pan. Spread sliced green onions over the broccoli. Over

Broccoli (*Brassica oleracea*, var.).

the onion sprinkle anchovies, broken into pieces, and over the anchovies break Romano or Parmesan cheese. Put another layer of broccoli over this and repeat the layers of onion, anchovies and cheese. This may be repeated as often as desired but there should be at least two layers of the ingredients. Pour a glass of red wine over all and add the oil from the anchovies. Cover and place a weight on the lid to keep the steam in the pan. Steam very slowly for 15 - 20 minutes. Do not add salt. When ready to serve, remove the lid, place a plate face down over the pan. Turn the pan into the plate. The broccoli, onions, anchovies and cheese will form a pie. Slice, and serve 4 - 6.

2 bunches of broccoli

Green onions

Anchovies

Romano or Parmesan cheese

A glass of red wine

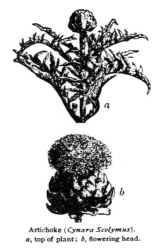

Artichoke (*Cynara Scolymus*).
a, top of plant; *b*, flowering head.

FELIX RUVULO 🎵 FRIED SICILIAN ARTICHOKES Snap off the leaves of the artichokes, leaving the tender, succulent base. Slit. Slice the base into about $\frac{1}{2}$ inch slices, cutting from top to bottom. Take out the furry, inedible part. Boil the slices until they are almost done. Mix French bread crumbs, finely-chopped garlic and parsley and grated

219

Romano cheese. Roll the slices of artichoke in this mixture. Fry in hot oil. Allow one artichoke per serving.

Artichokes

French bread crumbs

Garlic

Parsley

Romano cheese

Oil

TERRY FROST ℥ LEEKS A LA CORNWALL Heat a flat, round pan and melt butter or margarine. Add salt and pepper. Slice the leeks in rings to evenly cover the bottom of the pan. Cover. They are done as soon as they are tender, and may be served hot or cold. If served cold, a little vinegar may be added.

Leek.

Editors' note: The leek is the floral emblem of Wales, but it is equally respected in Cornwall. It is distinguished by membership in the lily family.

220

RATATOUILLE

221

KAY BOYLE ❧ **RATATOUILLE ROWAYTON** There is always a question as to whether a woman should or should not reveal the secrets which distinguish her. I do not know the answer entirely, but I do know that I am as loath to receive guests without my earrings on as I am to have my guests sit down to dinner without having my Ratatouille Rowayton in the oven with a generous sprinkling of freshly-grated Parmesan cheese encrusting the top. I have never divulged the recipe for this dish, and I do not intend to do so now. But put the depicted ingredients together, and you will have prepared one of the most satisfactory casseroles that ever accompanied a meat dish (preferably broiled chicken or baked ham), or — with fresh, briefly-boiled shrimp added — ever constituted an entire dinner in itself.

In either case, a garden of raw peas, lettuce and spinach leaves, tossed with olive oil, garlic salt, and lemon juice, must be present, as fresh and inevitable as apple blossoms in May.

1.

White and long-grained
and beloved in China.

2.

Drab green, hearts of,
and they may be frozen,
their natural habitat,
France or Italy.

3.

Emerald green and
varnished (come in red,
if you prefer).

222

4.

Bright red, and should be skinned for participation in the Ratatouille.

5.

Green, mottled like snakes. They might be taken for cucumbers by the undiscerning.

6.

Golden, and filled with forest darkness and evening dew. Take a squirrel's advice on the edible varieties.

5 must first be washed slightly in cold water, hand-dried, and sliced.

3 must be gutted of seeds and chopped fine.

2 may be split in two, broken hearts being more tender than others.

Now boil 1, 2, 3, 4, and 5 in a minimum of salted water for precisely fifteen minutes.

Remove from fire and add 6, which has been previously broiled in butter. Place entire mixture in a glass casserole so that the colors show, sprinkle with Parmesan, and place in middle of oven. Bake at 350° for fifteen minutes, broil for time required to brown the Parmesan. Serve with Beaujolais, 1959.

MARY SCOTT ♫ RATATOUILLE WITH EGGPLANT Heat some olive oil in a heavy saucepan and cook the sliced onions and the sliced, deseeded pimientos for about 5 minutes. Then add the sliced zucchini, the skinned and diced eggplant and the sliced mushrooms. Lastly add the tomatoes and a crushed clove of garlic and salt and pepper to taste. Cover tightly and cook very gently for half an hour. Mix the vegetables together without mashing them and cook another 15 or 20 minutes with the cover off. Pour off excess liquid before serving. Sprinkle with grated cheese. May be served cold. Serves 6.

2 or 3 onions, sliced

2 or 3 red or green pimientos, sliced and deseeded

2 unpeeled zucchini, sliced

3 or 4 tomatoes, skinned and sliced

2 eggplant, skinned and diced

$\frac{1}{4}$ pound mushrooms, sliced

Clove of garlic

Olive oil

Salt and pepper to taste

BEAUFORD DELANEY ♫ PEPPER TOUEE *Creole Ratatouille* Sauté the sliced onions and the garlic in olive oil. Add the tomatoes, peppers, vinegar and spices and cook tightly covered for about half an hour. Serves 4.

4 tomatoes, sliced

6 large green peppers, sliced

6 large onions, sliced

1 cup olive oil

½ teaspoon wine vinegar

4 garlic cloves

Thyme and salt, to taste

1 bay leaf

Large Bell Pepper.

226

RICE AND OTHER GRAINS

227

UPTON SINCLAIR ℒ MY LIFE IN RICE Some thirty years ago I published an article entitled "My Life in Diet." I got letters about it from all over the world and some said it was the funniest story they ever read. There is a lot more to the story now, and it has a happy ending; but I hope that won't spoil the fun.

I began as a small boy in Baltimore with sausage and flannel cakes with syrup for breakfast and fried chicken with fried mush for dinner. But my father was one of those old-fashioned Southern gentlemen who "drank," and so when I came to New York I was poor, and at the age of sixteen in City College I was earning my food by writing jokes and sketches. At eighteen I went up to Columbia as a special student and by then I was writing half-dime novels and keeping two stenographers busy dictating to them on alternate nights. After three years of this I figured that I had produced and had published an amount of wordage equal to the works of Sir Walter Scott. At the same time I had taken half a dozen graduate courses each year and had taught myself to read German, French, and Italian.

So it should be easy to understand that I had some stomach trouble. I went to a doctor, and he gave me a pink liquid that he said would help to digest my food. Maybe it did so but only for a time. I got the idea it might be something I was eating that caused the trouble, and I asked the doctor. He didn't think much of the idea and told me to go on eating what everybody else ate. For I don't know how many years I went on consulting doctors, but I never found one who had any interest in the idea that there could be anything wrong with the ordinary American diet.

But then somebody gave me a "health" magazine, what the doctors called a "crank" publication. It was *Physical Culture,* and I fell for it and began trying diets. There was the raw food diet and it was wonderful except that when I was doing brainwork I couldn't digest it. And there was the Salisbury meat diet — I tried that out while I was wintering in Fairhope, Alabama, and an old friend showed up there and wrote back to the *New Leader* in New York that he had found "the vegetarian Upton Sinclair living on stewed beefsteaks." I spent a month or two at the Battle Creek "San" and let the late Dr. Kellogg feed me his fancy grain products — which you now find in all the groceries. Next year I went to Macfadden's institution, which was just across the street, and let him put me on a fast and milk diet — which to Dr. Kellogg was high treason especially when I wrote a book called *The Fasting Cure*.

It really was an extraordinary experience: the feeling of lightness, of clearheadedness. I think it was twelve days that I fasted and thereafter, whenever I lectured about health, I could send an audience into gales of laughter by telling them how I had gone for a stroll with my wife and had come back to the building in which my room was located. It was on a slight rise of land, and I had to send my wife in to get me a lemon before I had sufficient strength to mount that rise.

In course of time I realized why I had got along so well in these various experiments — I was resting. The moment I got back to hard brainwork all my digestive troubles came back. In Pasadena I took to playing tennis. I had read that in the armies of King Cyrus it was the law that every soldier had to sweat every day. I made it a rule to sweat three or four times every week, and the scales showed that I sweated as much as five pounds of water in a hard-fought match. I lived on beefsteak, turnip greens, whole-wheat bread and fruit, and on that basis wrote a dozen books. But I had several breakdowns.

Rather oddly, I made the discovery that when I ran for governor of California, in the so-called EPIC campaign of 1934, I had no trouble at all — even though I was often addressing large audiences two or three times a day. The reason was that I enjoyed it and took it lightly; it was like saying lessons I had been learning for thirty years. There is no strain like creative writing in which you put your whole being into the souls of imaginary characters — for hours, for days and nights, for months, for years. That was the case with the eleven Lanny Budd books in which I lived for a dozen years. People write and ask me to make it a dozen books, but I shake my head.

Almost seven years ago, the lady who stood with me through these ordeals — and not enjoying them — suffered a grave heart attack. The doctors gave her the customary drugs, but she was failing fast. It happened that I read something about the rice diet, as advocated by Dr. Kempner of Duke University. I persuaded my wife and had her flown to a nearby city where a doctor consented to give her this diet. I don't name the city because I have to record that the hospital was badly run and my wife far from happy there. But the diet proved to be magical; after ten days or so she was able to walk up and down in the corridor, and several days later I persuaded her to let me take her to a little cottage a few miles away, take care of her myself, and bring her to the doctor twice a week.

So there I was, doctor's apprentice, nurse, chief cook and bottle washer for several months. She was living on rice, fruit, fruit juices, and vitamins — and doing so well that it was natural for me, lifelong health crank, to announce: "I'm going to cook an extra pot of rice for myself and see how it works." Craig was afraid but I went ahead, and my fate was decided in a few days. Call me a Hindu, call me a Jap, call me a Chinaman, call me anything you please — rice is the food for me. Just think of it: I, who for at least

The Panicle of Rice
(*Oryza sativa*).
a, a spikelet; *b*, the empty glumes; *c*, the flowering glume; *d*, the palet; *e*, the lodicules, the stamens, and the pistil.

forty years had been accustomed to saying that I was never more than twenty-four hours ahead of a headache, have not had a headache for seven years; and I am quietly confident that I shall never have another as long as I live — or as long as rice is grown in the Central California delta or imported from the Orient.

Seven years and a half works out at two thousand, five hundred and fifty-five days, plus half a day which is finishing while I write this. At three meals a day, that is eight thousand, six hundred and sixty-five. Twice in that period I recall having taken a visitor out to a hotel for lunch so that reduced the total. All the rest of the meals have been cooked by me, served by me, and eaten by me. My wife, alas, gave up the rice diet and slowly failed, had more heart attacks, and died.

As for me, I have what is called a sweet tooth, and all my meals are dessert and nothing else. I am writing this paragraph after supper, and that supper was as follows, all of it in one aluminum bowl: two Japanese persimmons, dead ripe, each as big as my fist; two lumps of cold boiled brown rice, as big as the persimmons; one heaping teaspoon of dried milk powder; one teaspoon of corn oil; as much lecithin as you could put on a penny; and, poured over the mixture, a glass of pineapple juice, fresh out of the icebox. With this I eat half a dozen pieces of well-washed celery, and take one all-purpose vitamin pill. If I am still hungry, I eat a couple of dates or a graham cracker or a teaspoon full of chocolate-milk powder.

Of course the fruit varies with the season. I am writing from California in January and it is persimmons, ripe bananas, and winter pears; later it will be peaches, berries and grapes, then figs and melons. I may open a can of fruit once in a month. I never drink water, and one large can of pineapple juice does me for a day. (I no longer play tennis; instead I take care of flowers and shrubs.) Because a doctor worried me with the idea that I was not getting enough protein, I added a little packet of gelatine to my noon meal — which I call lunch since I could not dignify it with the term dinner.

The only disadvantage of this diet is that you can't get it in a restaurant or in any other person's home. But since I have to choose between sociability with headaches and solitude without, I have chosen the latter. To prepare the meals and clear up afterwards takes less than half an hour of my time, and I am happy not to have a stranger in the house. I drive to the post office twice a day and do the shopping. When I am tired, I lie down and read. I take some fifty magazines, and I watch the world that way. It is not a happy world, but I live on hope.

This is a book about diet, so I conclude: I am 83, am 5 feet 7, and keep my weight at 130 to 135. I repeat the all-important statement that during those almost seven years I have not had an ache or a pain of any character. (I knock on wood!)

BARNEY WAN ∫ CHINESE RICE Prepare the rice with two parts water to one part rice, or add water to the desired amount of rice until it reaches the joints of fingers to hand when the hand is placed flat in the pan on top of the rice. Bring to a fast boil, then simmer until all the water is gone. *Do not stir.*

YEKTAI ∫ PERSIAN RICE Prepare ½ cup of rice per person. Place rice in salted, boiling water until the rice grains are soft on the edges but hard in the middle. (They may be tested by pinching a grain between thumb and fingernail.) Remove from fire and drain the rice. Add a tablespoon of butter. Allow the butter to melt, then add about a teaspoon of water. Return the rice to the fire. Cover with a clean, dry, absorbent cloth. Cook on as low a fire as possible for about 45 minutes. The cloth will absorb the moisture and the rice near the bottom of the pan will brown and become crisp. Add more butter just before serving.

EPHREM WEITZMAN ∫ POPPY SEED RICE Prepare rice or use leftover boiled rice. Brown onions, sliced or chopped, mushrooms and a clove of garlic. Add the rice and poppy seeds. Mix, cook briefly and serve. Canned tuna fish can be added in the browning stage.

232

Rice
Onions
Mushrooms
Garlic
Poppy seeds
Optional: tuna fish

MERVIN JULES ☙ KASHA (*Kasha*: groats: grits: coarse cracked wheat or the edible parts of oat kernels.) Fry a cup of chopped onions until they are a golden brown.

In a mixing bowl, beat one egg for each cup of *kasha*. Add the *kasha* to the egg. Salt to taste. Heat and dissolve ½ cup of chicken fat or, lacking that, butter.

Add the chopped, browned onions and the *kasha* mixture to the melted fat, stirring constantly. Add a good deal of water, little by little, for the desired consistency. Cook for a quarter of an hour, adding water; then lower the flame and steam, covered.

1 cup chopped onions for 2 cups *kasha*
1 egg for each cup *kasha*
Salt
½ cup melted chicken fat or butter

Editors' note: Kasha *expands greatly in the cooking. Consider well the end. One cup of* kasha, *when cooked, becomes (roughly) four.*

SALADS AND SALAD DRESSINGS

235

A. COSTA 𝔖 SALADE NICOISE & ACCOMPANIMENTS Cooking is my hobby and color my delight, and therefore I try to combine tasty, many-hued menus when I wish to entertain a few friends. For a small party of six or eight I would first serve a *Salade Niçoise,* which can be prepared in advance and will not suffer if any of the guests are late.

To make it first steam two cupfuls of rice being careful not to overcook the rice as the grains must remain detached and slightly cracking as for a Turkish pilaff. Set the rice aside to cool and, meanwhile, slice coarsely a couple of large, fresh red peppers and two green ones. Then dice one big cucumber, having removed the rind. To these basic ingredients you may add any bright vegetables that catch your fancy — raw peas, diced carrots, salted runner beans, etc. A few shelled prawns might add an unexpected flavour to the dish.

Now prepare a one-egg mayonnaise with salt, pepper, one teaspoonful of wine vinegar and enough olive oil — added drop by drop — to keep your sauce on the rather thin side. Once the rice is cold, fold in the various ingredients and pour the mayonnaise on top. Mix the salad thoroughly.

For the main course one or several wild fowl would do nicely — pheasant or duck, partridge, woodcock or grouse, according to taste and season. Wrap them in thin slices of bacon and roast in a moderate oven, basting frequently. The time to cook the birds will naturally depend on their size as will the carving, the smaller ones being halved, the larger ones carved like any back-yard fowl.

Bread crumbs and chipped potatoes might accompany the roast and a bowl of crisp, bright green, young lettuce. Toss this with a French dressing of salt, pepper, lemon juice and olive oil (avoid ready-made salad creams like the plague) and sprinkle with finely-scented herbs: chives, fennel, parsley, thyme, mint and the like, so that it doesn't clash with your first course.

For a sweet, a black-currant fool made of preserved fruit whipped in the electric mixer with half a pint of thick cream and plenty of sugar. This will add an unusual note of purple to the multi-colored dinner party.

An assortment of international cheeses can conclude the meal, if desired, and I would recommend a judicious choice of French wines.

Salade Niçoise:
2 cups of rice
2 red peppers
2 green peppers
1 cucumber
Peas, diced carrots, prawns (optional)
1 egg
Salt, pepper
Wine vinegar
Olive oil

JOAN NEUHOF  **RICE SALAD** For cold precooked rice (½ cup per person) make a sauce of olive oil, salt, pepper, crushed garlic or garlic juice, mustard (either dry or prepared) and a little vinegar. Add onion, sliced green pepper, tomatoes and chunk tuna fish. For a heartier salad, sliced hard-boiled eggs and black olives may be added.

Cold cooked rice
Olive oil
Salt

Pepper

Crushed garlic or garlic juice

Mustard (dry or prepared)

1, part of the inflorescence of mustard (*Brassica nigra*). 2, a leaf. *a*, flower cut longitudinally, the petals removed. *b*, a pod.

Vinegar

Onion

Green pepper

Tomatoes

Chunk tuna fish

———◆———

JERRE MANGIONE ✥ ITALIAN PASSION SALAD This is *not* an aphrodisiac for underheated Indians, as its name might imply. It is more closely related to overheated ones since its inventor was a passionate patriot, a follower of Garibaldi during

238

the Great Liberator's Sicilian campaign. He was one of my ancestors who served under Garibaldi as a cook. The story goes that Gasparo Mangione ran out of meat one day and in his anxiety to provide a vegetable dish which was worthy of Garibaldi, he combined three ingredients the colors of which form the Italian flag: tomatoes (thinly-sliced), potatoes (boiled, cold, thickly-sliced) and string beans (boiled, cold). To give this alliance its moment of truth he added a sliced Italian onion.

The salad proved to be a burping success, and its fame quickly spread through Sicily and southern Italy. At first it may have been served as a patriotic gesture but now it is widely consumed as a gastronomic delight, one which, when served with Italian bread, can make a satisfying meal by itself.

As prepared by my family the string beans comprise about half of the salad. More or less equal parts of boiled potatoes and sliced tomatoes make up the balance. Unless you are a wrestler or a misanthrope, one medium-sized raw onion is usually enough in a salad for two. The dressing should be as simple as possible: three parts olive oil, one part wine vinegar and some salt and pepper.

Toss, eat, and thank your stars for passionate Italians.

Tomatoes
Potatoes, boiled
String beans, boiled
Italian onion
Olive oil
Wine vinegar
Salt and pepper

239

FRANCES PARKINSON KEYES ✒ CREAM OF CUCUMBER SALAD*

Soften the gelatin in the cold water, add the hot milk and stir until the gelatin is dissolved. Add the remaining ingredients and mix well. Turn the salad into a mold and chill in the refrigerator for 12 hours. Serve on lettuce leaves with French dressing. Serves 6.

This salad dates back to my New England bride days. I took it to the Senate luncheon when we entertained for Cabinet ladies, and everyone said it was the best salad ever served there. I had so many requests for this recipe that I had it printed on cards and gave it away for Christmas greetings.

Improved Long Green Cucumber.

2 teaspoons gelatin

2 tablespoons cold water

¼ cup hot milk

1 cucumber, cut into small cubes

1 cup heavy cream, whipped

½ sweet pimiento, chopped

1 teaspoon tarragon vinegar

Salt and lemon juice to taste

*From the Frances Parkinson Keyes Cookbook.

W. L. WHITE ⌇ A FEW MILD REMARKS ON TOSSED SALADS You can put almost anything tasty in them except watery gunk like sliced tomatoes, for it is necessary that everything first be thoroughly dried and this you can do yourself by pressing each lettuce leaf gently with a folded towel as between the leaves of a book.

The second tip is that raw mushrooms are completely delicious in them. Use plenty — at least a quarter of a pound. They are better sliced — about as thick as your little finger or thick enough to make a respectable bite.

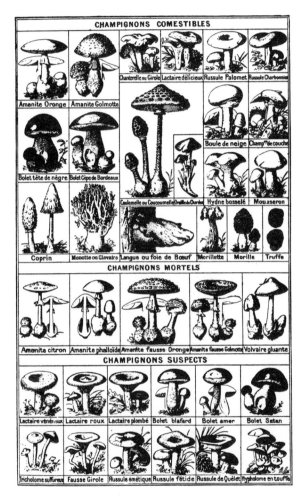

From here on out, we get into a serious difference of opinion. My wife, who picked up this trick of using raw mushrooms in salads while we were in Italy, feels that mushrooms should be peeled — or at least washed — by holding them quickly under a running cold-water faucet and then drying them, for, she points out, the best of them are raised in humid beds of pig manure.

I contend that most of a mushroom's flavor (and probably vitamins) is in the skin, which peeling removes; that pig manure has been the victim of a bad press; and anyway, very little could possibly be left by the time the mushroom arrives in the supermarket. Finally, what the guests don't know won't hurt them, so that, if a few golden flakes do remain their flavor is usually mistaken by the guests for that of a dash of soy sauce, and in consequence heartily praised by them. I realize, however, that in these decadent democratic days my wife will have the weight of numbers on her side — all of them frantically peeling their mushrooms in quaking dread of pig manure. With me will be only a tiny, dwindling but devoted band of dedicated gourmets.

Then, after the leaves and mushrooms have been thoroughly coated with oil — not so much that it drips but enough to give each leaf the shine of a factory-fresh compact — salt the salad to taste.

Now how about other flavorings? A number of herbs are excellent. Black pepper is

Black Pepper (*Piper nigrum*). Long Pepper (*Piper longum*).

standard. A touch of curry powder, marjoram, cumin, oregano, or pressed garlic clove (but beware of too much) — all are delicious. You will find it fun to vary them.

Wine vinegar or lemon juice? The best Italian cooks never use them, and I have found they are right. Their strong bite completely kills the delicate herb flavors.

ARTHUR DESHAIES ꧁ A NEW ENGLAND APRIL SALAD

Dandelion leaves, with tight silver buds, preferably picked dewed
A handful of rhubarb shoots, diced
A bouquet of the top young leaves of milkweed
A small corsage of the youngest leaves of violet and white clover
A half-dozen very young sweet fiddleheads
Six cowlicks of sour grass

Make a dressing of ò*lio raffinato,*
a sssss-z-t of lemon juice,
and sprinkle
(before mixing)
with monosodium glutamate.

Editors' note: Those fiddleheads and sour grass recall Ralph Waldo Emerson's tolerant definition of a weed: "A plant whose virtues have not yet been discovered." (Fortune of the Republic)

RALPH STACKPOLE ꧁ SALADE AUVERGNATE DE PISSENLITS Gather

about 5 ounces of dandelions, choosing greens that are partially white. Wash thoroughly. Dry. Add 2 tablespoons of walnut oil, 2 tablespoons of white wine vinegar, salt and pepper to taste and one grated clove of garlic. Cut two hard-boiled eggs into cubes and add

243

to the greens. If walnut oil is not available fry a few slices of bacon, cutting it into very small pieces. Pour the hot oil and bacon bits over the salad. This will give the greens a different flavour. Serves 4.

Pissenlit.

5 ounces of dandelion greens

2 tablespoons of walnut oil (or hot bacon oil and bacon bits)

2 tablespoons of white wine vinegar

Salt, pepper

Garlic

2 hard-boiled eggs

HARRISON McINTOSH   SALADE VINAIGRETTE

1 part wine vinegar with garlic

4 parts peanut oil

About 1 tablespoon garlic salt

1 teaspoon plain salt

1 teaspoon coarsely-ground pepper

1½ tablespoons French mustard

One little squeeze of lemon

Mix well and beat with a fork. Let stand, covered for half an hour. Beat with a fork again, let stand another half an hour and beat again. This tastes better the next day; shake well before using.

This makes enough for four or five average salads and is ideal for a plain French salad of butter lettuce.

WALTER EDMONDS ⌁ SAUCE PIQUANTE The first requisite is a good bed of chervil so that one sauce will not exhaust the supply. Pick two or three double handfuls of chervil and chop it finely to more or less fill a quart-sized bowl. Chop or rice two large hard-boiled eggs and place on top of the chervil. Make a sour French dressing, using white wine tarragon vinegar as follows:

Place in a salad spoon two small salt spoonfuls of salt. Add freshly-ground black pepper until the salt and pepper, when mixed, appear to be of equal quantities. Add paprika of equal quantity to the salt and pepper mixture and add about a salt spoonful of dry English mustard. Mix the paprika and the mustard into the salt and pepper, then add the vinegar to fill the salad spoon and stir until the salt and pepper appear to be dissolved. Scatter this mixture over the egg and chervil, add three salad spoonfuls of olive oil, stir together until the egg is evenly mixed throughout the chervil.

This, unlike the *sauce piquante* which is ordinarily offered in restaurants — a thin affair — produces a thick paste which can be spread with a knife. There is nothing better with cold lamb, beef (especially cold sirloin steak) or even chicken.

ELISE CAVANNA ⌘ COOL GREEN SALAD DRESSING* Certain mixtures would be impossible without a blender — this is one of them. Blend these four ingredients and chill the results. Serve over crisp lettuce. Through the green pepper, this sauce delivers a large dose of vitamin C.

¾ cup peeled, diced green pepper

½ cup low-fat cottage cheese

1 heaping teaspoon honey

1 package George Washington Golden Broth powder

*From Gourmet Cookery for a Low-Fat Diet.

HIDETAKA OHNO ⌘ THE PICKLES — AUTUMN

Egg apples (small ones more delicious!)

Green beefsteak plants (leaves and berries)

Red cayenne pepper

*Zingiber mioga**

Dry the vegetables out in the shade a day or two before pickling. Do not dry the green beefsteak too much. Pickle (with salt only) each material separately a week, and pickle them altogether again. Wonderful sake and the eatables!

A Few Words:
Art is a sex act.
Nature is like the feminine sex.
Either she calls on you or you set out.
"Well, then, let's go out."
"You, too, please."

*Ginger.

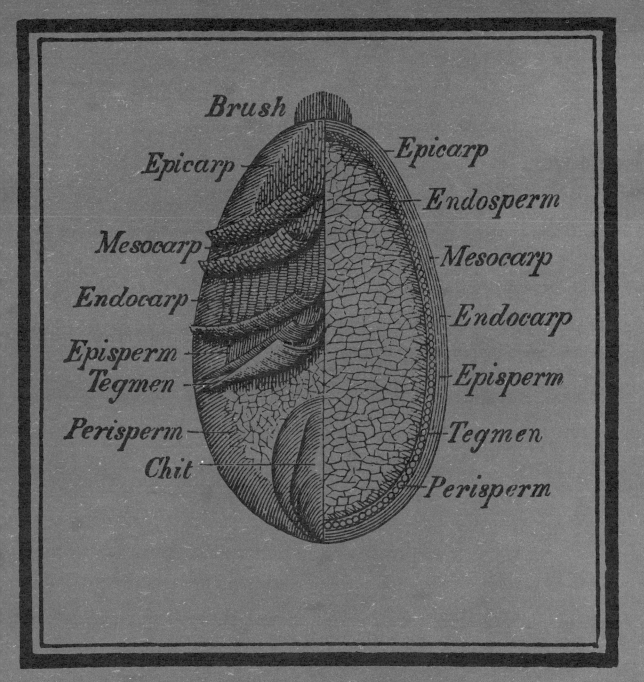

Brush

Epicarp

Mesocarp

Endocarp

Episperm
Tegmen

Perisperm

Chit

Epicarp

Endosperm

Mesocarp

Endocarp

Episperm

Tegmen

Perisperm

BREADS

247

MALCOLM BRADBURY 🎺 A RECIPE FOR YORKSHIRE PUDDING The ritual associated with Yorkshire pudding is, of course, a class one. American recipes are about violence and identity, just as are American novels and American life. English recipes are all about class, just as are English novels and English life. Yorkshire pudding is then not only a regional recipe but a working-class one, and this is the rationale for my way (the proper way, that is) of preparing it. But first I should explain that Yorkshire is, of course, in the North Country, a part of England known for its friendliness and good fellowship. The South of England is the part that is stuffy and reserved, given to supping fancy, fizzy drinks and living the smart life. The North is provincial and takes a pride in it. Thus the East Riding of Yorkshire has the only buses in England with Gothic-pointed roofs. This is because towns like York and Beverley are still walled and battlemented in case of invasion from the South, and the buses have to have special roofs in the Gothic style to negotiate the Gothic gateways to the towns. The East Riding is largely rural, but the West Riding is industrial. It is the Riding of J. B. Priestley and John Braine. And the West Riding is the true home of Yorkshire pudding. I was born in the West Riding and now live in the East, so I have fidelities to both; but I have to admit that the West makes the best Yorkshire pudding.

The reason for this is that Yorkshire pudding is essentially an economical dish. Many slovenly habits have grown up around the Yorkshire pudding, but the real, the honest, fully-integrated Yorkshire pudding is, in fact, served not with roast beef but preceding it. Real Yorkshire pudding experts, the working-class housewives of Bradford, Leeds and Sheffield, know that its purpose is to prevent anyone wanting the roast beef at all.

248

It is a substitute for it and not an accompaniment to it; it is to make the meat last until another day and, therefore, the dish cannot be truly appreciated without a certain degree of poverty. The distinctive quality of Yorkshire pudding is, indeed, that it is filling though it is also nourishing and subtle in its flavours (some cooks vary the basic taste by adding onions or herbs). It is also nourishing. One of the main sources of the flavour and the nourishment comes from the fact that it should always be placed in the oven beneath the roasting meat in such a way that the juices from the meat (which is placed on a rack above) drip into it. In wintertime, in order to make the puddings lighter, Yorkshire ladies take two tablespoonfuls of freshly-fallen snow and stir it into the mixture just before putting it into the oven.

Here, then, is my wife's recipe for:

Yorkshire Pudding (for Yorkshire authors and Angry Young Men): Sift the flour and salt in a basin (leaving room at the top). Hollow out the centre with the back of a wooden (Wood in) spoon, then drop in the whole unbeaten egg. Add 2 tablespoonfuls of the milk, then beat milk and egg together with the wooden spoon. Gradually draw in flour from the sides, beating all the time. As you beat you will find the flour falls in almost of its own accord. Add more milk *gradually,* beating all the time so that lumps do not form. When slightly more than half the liquid has been beaten in — and all the flour — beat well with a wooden spoon for 5 - 10 minutes. The surface must be well covered with bubbles.

Stir in the rest of the milk and stand in a cool place for about an hour.

Roast a joint of beef. Thirty minutes before the meat is ready turn up your oven to 400° F. When the oven is heated to this temperature drain off all but about three tablespoonfuls of fat and meat dripping, leaving enough to cover the bottom of the pan. Some cooks have the pudding above on a rack while others float the pudding around the meat. Pour in the pudding batter and return to the oven. Cook for about 25 minutes, or until the pudding is risen and set.

Serve on hot plates with rich gravy as an entree to fill people up so that they won't eat too much meat. If you like slightly heavier pudding, pour in the batter about *one hour* before the meat is ready and cook in a moderate oven until meat and pudding are ready. The beef is cooked in the usual way, save that the English prefer theirs well hung, unrefrigerated and well- if not overcooked. Yorkshire pudding for 4.

————————◆————————

4 oz. plain flour

¼ teaspoonful salt

1 egg

½ pint milk

————————◆————————

Wheat (*Triticum sativum*).
1, the complete plant of the variety *æstivum;* 2, the spike of the same; 3, the spike of the variety *hibernum;* 4, a grain germinating. *a*, part of the rachis; *b*, the floret of the variety *æstivum; c*, the flower, showing two lodicules, the stamens, and the stigmas.

250

GWEN DAVENPORT ✍ CASSEROLE BREAD Writers as cooks have one great advantage over cooks who work away from home. As the G.I. said of the Australian girls, "It's not what they've got but that they've got it *here*."

Dissolve yeast in 1 cup lukewarm water (test on wrist). Sift flour, sugar and salt together in large bowl. Stir in dissolved yeast. Add just enough of the extra water to hold dough together. Dough should be soft and sticky when mixed. Cover with cloth and set bowl in kitchen (not near direct heat) and let rise until double in size (2 to 4 hours depending on warmth of kitchen). For dinner at 7, start bread at noon.

When dough is high and spongy, punch it down with fist and beat it soundly with hand. Divide in two parts and place each in a greased 6″ round baking dish or glass casserole. Cover again with cloth and let rise until it reaches the top of the dish. (Again about 3 hours.) Start the oven at 400°, brush the top of the bread with melted butter and bake for one hour. Serve hot, cut in six wedges. Second loaf may be kept frozen. To use it, moisten slightly, wrap in foil and heat.

This is the nearest thing I know to French, Italian or Mexican bread. There is no country in the world that does not have better bread than the United States.

--------●--------

1 package quick-acting yeast
4 cups (after sifting) all-purpose flour
1½ cups lukewarm water
1 tablespoon sugar
1 tablespoon salt

--------●--------

HARPER LEE ✍ CRACKLING BREAD First, catch your pig. Then ship it to the *abattoir* nearest you. Bake what they send back. Remove the solid fat and throw the rest away. Fry fat, drain off liquid grease, and combine the residue (called "cracklings") with:

1½ cups water-ground white meal

1 teaspoon salt

1 teaspoon baking powder

1 egg

1 cup milk

Bake in very hot oven until brown (about 15 minutes).

Result: one pan crackling bread serving 6. Total cost: about $250, depending upon size of pig. Some historians say by this recipe alone fell the Confederacy.

JOHN KNOWLES 𝔖 BAPTIST CAKE This requires no hashish and has never been heard of at the *Cordon Bleu;* no coffee house has ever served it. It is just a simple West Virginia mountain dish my mother (of course) used to make.

Butter a skillet lightly and heat to medium degree. Roll bread dough about ¼ inch thick. Prick dough several times with a fork. Fry a few minutes on one side and a few on the other. Serve immediately with plenty of butter.

VERNON WATKINS 𝔖 FRIED LAVER BREAD (BARA LAWR) Wash the seaweed well to remove sand, then boil five times until all traces of sand are gone. Mix with fine oatmeal and form into small cakes. Fry in bacon fat and serve with bacon and fried bread. For best flavor, gather the fine, glossy laver yourself from the rocks at low tide. A mile of laver produces approximately three cubic inches of itself fried.

Several miles of seaweed*

Fine oatmeal

Bacon fat

ANTHONY WEST 🜊 OLD-FASHIONED BREAD A good bread to eat with soup or comb honey or jam is easily made by the following method:

Take one pound of fine ground whole-wheat flour and one pound of coarse ground whole-wheat flour and two to four ounces of cracked wheat and a heaping tablespoonful of salt. Mix all together in a large bowl and set aside in a warm place. Now, liberally butter a bread tin, making sure that its bottom and sides are well greased, going carefully into the corners. Then take one and a half ounces of yeast and two and a half teaspoonfuls of dark brown sugar and work them into a paste with a little warm water in the bottom of a measure which will take at least a pint. When you have your paste, add warm water till you have a pint of liquid. Take a wooden spoon and work this liquid into the mixed flour until you have a strong elastic dough which will roll out of the bowl and into the bread tin in one piece. All flours are not equally absorbent and some may need more water than others before the dough becomes an elastic mass — up to a pint and a half may be needed. It is a mistake to add water after the dough has become work-

*Green laver (Ulva latissima or lactuca), sea lettuce; or red laver (Porphyra laciniata or vulgaris)

253

able as a weak dough will rise too much and give trouble in the oven by pouring over the edges of the tin. When the dough has been rolled out of the bowl and into the tin, it should be covered with a cloth and left to rise in a warm place out of all drafts. At the end of forty minutes or an hour the dough will have risen. It should then be standing half an inch or more above the top of the tin in a rounded shape. It should now be put in an oven ready at a temperature of 400 degrees. In fifty minutes to an hour the loaf will be ready. A metal skewer pushed in through the crust will come out cleanly without any attached dough when it is properly done. The loaf should be left to stand in its tin for five minutes before any attempt to turn it out is made. If it is hurried it will break up. At the end of five minutes a knife blade should be worked round between the crust and the tin until the loaf can be gently levered out. It should be put to cool in some rack or openwork shelf where the air can get at its underside. The result is a good crusty old-fashioned bread which does not have to be toasted to be made eatable.

————— ◆ —————

One pound fine ground whole-wheat flour
One pound coarse whole-wheat flour
Two to four ounces of cracked wheat
A heaped tablespoonful of salt
Butter
One and a half ounces of yeast
Two and a half teaspoonfuls of dark brown sugar

————— ◆ —————

SIR SHANE LESLIE 🔱 IRISH BROWN BREAD Sift flour, salt, soda and sugar in a basin. Rub the butter into the meal. Mix all together.

Make a hole in centre of the flour and pour in ½ to ¾ pint sour milk. Stir well and make a soft dough. Knead lightly. Cut a cross on top and bake for 45 to 50 minutes in a fairly-hot oven.

8 ounces whole or wheaten meal

8 ounces flour

1 level teaspoon salt

$\frac{3}{4}$ pint sour milk

1 ounce butter

$1\frac{1}{2}$ teaspoons baking soda

1 teaspoon sugar

Butter Worker.

ALEXANDRE ISTRATI ♫ POLENTA A LA ROUMANIE In a large, heavy pot bring about a quart and a half of water to boil. Add salt and then, little by little, finely-ground corn meal, stirring *constantly* and slowly with a wooden baton. When the corn meal mixture is the consistency of cereal, add no more corn meal, but continue to stir on a very low fire for ¾ hour. It will gradually thicken. When the wooden baton can stand erect in the mixture, remove the pan from the fire. Continue to stir for 5 to 6 minutes, allowing the polenta to cool slightly. Then turn the fire very high. Return the polenta to the fire for no more than one minute, then turn the pan out onto a platter, preferably a wooden one. The polenta will retain the shape of the pan. Serve with poached eggs, butter, soft white cheeses (Roquefort, Cantal, Boursin, etc.) and sour cream. Or serve with chicken. Serves 6 - 8.

1½ quarts boiling water

Salt

About 2 cups ground corn meal

Editors' note: This recipe for polenta, the bread of Roumanian peasantry, was taught to Alexandre Istrati by his fellow countryman and good friend, Constantin Brancusi.

JAMES BROOKS   REAL CORN BREAD   This recipe predates the nutritional enlightenment, contains no white flour, and belongs in the family of great breads. Mix:

Indian Corn.

2 cups corn meal

1 teaspoon baking soda

2 teaspoons salt

2 teaspoons baking powder

Mix separately:

2 eggs

4 tablespoons shortening (melted butter or vegetable oil or bacon fat)

2 cups buttermilk

Preheat oven to 450 degrees. Put large iron skillet (regular or enameled) in oven till it is hot. Mix dry and wet ingredients. Grease the skillet, pour in the batter, and bake from 20 to 30 minutes. Serve in pie-shaped slices, well-buttered. Ten slices.

The foregoing is a double recipe so there will be enough corn bread left over to make this wonderful dish which can serve instead of potatoes, rice, etc.

JAMES BROOKS ⌘ CUSH OF CORN BREAD Barely cover 2 or 3 slices of corn bread in a skillet with water. For each slice of corn bread add:

1 finely-chopped medium onion

1 tablespoon butter or shortening

Cook down on a medium heat, stirring frequently, until the cush loses any pasty consistency and is almost dry. Salt and pepper to taste. For four.

STREETER BLAIR ⌘ ORANGE BREAD Took Sunday drive, stopped at Ramona, California, cafe, saw sign "Homemade bread," ordered some, ate it, liked same. Got recipe from ranch woman running cafe. Baked a batch, turned out good, someone said, "Enter loaf at County Fair, Pomona, California." Baked white, also whole-wheat and all whole-wheat. Won three firsts. Newspaper ran story, women all over country wrote in for recipe. Wrote long letters explaining. Another ranch woman said, "Have orange bread recipe." Paid dollar for recipe, baked orange bread for same fair next year. Got first for orange bread and other firsts and ribbons on nine kinds of bread. Didn't give out recipes on orange bread.

Had fire! Burned everything, didn't bake for nine months. Fair time, decided to bake again, but couldn't remember proportions on white bread and decided to look in cook-

257

book. Found same recipe I had used, in three books. Only one recipe for white bread, standard, anywhere. After this told women to look in cookbook. Decided that recipe for white bread had nothing to do with winning. Must have been how you do it. Figured out from judges' rating that it was appearance of bread that won for me. Texture, crumb, grain, odor, taste, baking, and appearance all counted. Appearance just 5%. Realized that I had always had one or two loaves of batch that did *not* crack out, or feather, along sides of loaf at top of pan. I had always sent such a loaf. Tried to get loaf that way but no success. Called Pillsbury, General Mills, Domestic Science schools at Universities, High Schools, Gas Company, Stove people and all had suggestions, but no results. Tried 38 batches, gave bread away, had no deepfreeze, and didn't know anyway if bread would be good after being frozen. Knowing that I *had* gotten perfect loaves before fire, without trying, couldn't understand why no perfect loaf on purpose.

Realized I had started painting, same time as baking bread, and because it's tiresome waiting three approximate one-hour periods for bread to rise I had always painted while bread was in bowl or pans. An hour in painting is 20 minutes, therefore there was no waiting for bread to rise. Had heard of touch system, to tell when to put bread in oven. Noted that at about 49 minutes the bread had slightly softened after rising in the pans and that at about 60 minutes it was so soft that when touched, the bread did not jump back, except very slowly. The rule had been to put bread in oven when bread sprung back slowly after touch. Had kept log in book on the 38 batches, four loaves each batch, as to timing and conditions of dough for each minute after 49 or 50 minutes in pan. Laboratory of General Mills told me bread would not crack out if left in pans one hour and one half. Tried this and there was no crack out, but grain of bread was coarse and would lose more than 5% for appearance, so that was out.

However, this did cause me to run log on touch system after the dough had relaxed in pan to point of slow return of stiffening. Ran log each minute on touch after 49 minutes on the four loaves and was amazed to find that after 58 or 60 minutes depending on room temperature etc. that the dough began to stiffen again. Placed loaves in oven at different stages of second stiffening of dough and got two perfect loaves, no crack or feathering.

It seems that about halfway on the retightening stage is the best. A lawyer called up and said he wanted to bake bread and could he come and take notes on what to do. He brought notebook, banana, and sandwich and noted each step. I told him when we got to the oven stage that the first loaf should crack considerably, the next two should be almost perfect and the fourth loaf should crack out. I was right. Too soon or too late lets the loaf crack or feather, but the intervening period gives excellent shape and retains the grain fineness.

Bought a secondhand deepfreeze and froze the second-grade loaf of whole-wheat bread one year. Always entered the first-grade loaf at the current Fair Show. Got first prize on the year-old loaf. Time magazine and radio-television-newspapers all over the world carried the news. In Paris a director of Standard Brands read the story and I was told by a secretary at the Directors' meeting in Chicago that the impact of frozen bread was discussed. Amana Freezer people gave me a big five-shelf freezer. Fleischmann's sends yeast ever since and Reynolds Aluminum sends foil because I had used that at times in the oven to stop browning of top of loaf. Also later I used foil for wrapping a loaf of nut bread in the freezer for a year. It got first, too. Then I put away a loaf of orange bread for *two* years, for people had said that flavor would be lost if flavor of fruit was used. Entered the two-year-old loaf of orange bread and got first again. The record was eight firsts in eight years at the Fair, for orange bread. In this case, I admit it is the recipe, not so much the doing that accounts for first prizes. This orange bread is really a joy to taste. No one has the recipe except Fleur Cowles in London. She gave me three pages on my painting when she was editor of *Look* magazine, May 18th, 1954. I don't bake bread for fairs anymore. No challenge; but I do about twice a year take a baking spree and fill the freezer with three or four kinds of staple bread and a few batches of orange bread for Christmas gifts, and of course at those times, since I run one batch of 6 loaves each right after another, there isn't much need for painting to make the time fly. Whether or not a loaf cracks out isn't important except for competition. The flavor of bread is the same regardless of the moment same is put into the oven. By the way, white bread is the only kind sensitive to this exact moment of putting in the oven. Any other bread because of heavier ingredients, I think, does not crack out if the general rule of putting the dough in the oven when it has started to relax in the pans is used. Below is the recipe and method for making *Orange Bread:*

Dissolve yeast in the water. Add orange juice, salt, one cup of flour and half of the sugar. Stir until smooth, cover, let rise until about double. Add remaining sugar, butter, grated peel, candied orange rind (reground once), yolk of egg, and most of remaining flour. Knead about 200 times; let rise until double, or until a soft touch leaves a dent. Ball and shape into a loaf, and put in the pan to rise again. Bake in a moderate (350°) oven about one hour. One loaf.

———— •—•• ————

1 envelope or cake of compressed yeast

1 cup orange juice

2 tablespoons grated orange peel

4 tablespoons sugar

2 tablespoons melted butter or Wesson Oil

$\frac{1}{2}$ cup candied orange peel

1 egg yolk

$\frac{1}{2}$ teaspoon salt

$\frac{1}{4}$ cup lukewarm water

$2\frac{1}{2}$ or nearly 3 cups flour

———— •—•• ————

I sometimes let the dough rise the second time in the bowl after punching down and turning after the first rise. I always bake four or more loaves. Three envelopes of yeast is sufficient for a four-loaf batch.

RELLA RUDOLPH ❦ AN UNLEAVENED BREAD Mix all dry ingredients and add egg white. Add cold water a little at a time until the mixture is supple enough to pour into a baking pan. Add a little cinnamon, zest of lemon and raisins if desired. Brush with the yellow of the egg to which a little sesame seed has been added. Bake.

7 tablespoons buckwheat flour

7 tablespoons oatmeal

7 tablespoons corn meal

2 tabiespoons sea salt (level)

7 tablespoons oil

1 egg

MAX STEELE ❦ GOOD BREAD Knead on floured surface until bubbles form beneath surface (8-12 minutes). Let rise in covered greased bowl in warm (90-100) area 2 to 3 hours. Poke down every time it becomes pregnant looking. Shape 2 loaves in greased pans. Cover and let rise again in warm place 2 hours. Bake at 325 degrees for about an hour.

Especially recommended to starving writers and artists. It has as much protein as many meats, as much vitamin B as many pills, is easy to make while working. Tastes like bread.

Soften: 1 packet dry yeast in

1 cup warm water

Combine: $\frac{1}{2}$ cup honey

1 tablespoon salt

2 tablespoons corn oil

1 cup warm water

Stir:

Add: softened yeast

Add gradually: $\frac{1}{4}$ cup brewers' yeast

$\frac{1}{2}$ cup wheat germ flour

$2\frac{1}{4}$ cups soy flour

3 cups white flour

EVAN HUNTER 🍳 PANCAKES You have to understand pancakes.

If you call them griddle cakes or flapjacks, you don't understand them and you might just as well forget ever trying to make them. Griddle cakes are made in restaurants that have shiny aluminum stoves and fake chefs in big white pastry hats; they have nothing whatever to do with pancakes which are made in people's kitchens. Flapjacks are made by gold prospectors in little wooden shacks in Grade-B movies; they also have nothing at all to do with pancakes. If you don't understand the distinction, then you won't understand pancakes, either. All is lost, and you should buy yourself a waffle iron.

You don't cook pancakes. You make them.

You don't say, "I think I'll cook some pancakes this morning." You always say, "I think I'll *make* some pancakes this morning." In fact, you never say that either because there's only one time to make pancakes and that's on Sunday morning, and you don't have to *think* you'll make them, you *know* you'll make them. That is, if you understand them. If you understand pancakes, you instinctively know they are irrevocably linked to Sunday morning, and sleeping late, and people in robes with sleep around the edges of their eyes and dopey sleep-smiles on their mouths as they suggest, "Why don't you make some pancakes?"

You'd make them anyway. This is Sunday morning.

Here's how you make them:

You buy yourself any one of the commercial mixes. Get yourself a big mixing bowl, a tablespoon, and a cup, and spread these out on the table. Now put the box where you can read the recipe. Sometimes, if you leave the box open after using it, you'll find cereal bugs in it the next time you try making pancakes. It's best to put the prepared mix in a container of some kind, but be sure to cut the recipe off the back of the box, or next time you won't know what you're doing.

The only change I make in the prepared mix recipe is to pour in about half a cup of heavy cream which, I find, gives the pancakes a richer taste and texture. Aside from that, pancakes shouldn't be tampered with. Don't go dropping diced apples into the batter, or blueberries, because then you're not making pancakes anymore. You're baking muffins or cakes.

Don't serve pancakes in any fancy way like putting ice cream on them or fruit, or brandy, or whipped cream. Just put a generous lump of butter on top of each pancake in the stack and then liberally pour either syrup or molasses over them. It isn't advisable to put more than four pancakes in a stack. Excessive depth makes them difficult to cut and difficult to handle on the fork. If you put four in a stack, you can serve two people while your next batch is on the griddle. Pancakes don't encourage simultaneous serving, but there's a lively overlap and, as a result, a built-in anticipation, especially when chil-

263

dren are sitting at the table waiting to be served. The cook always gets served last or, when the pancakes are especially successful, not at all. That doesn't matter.

What does matter is that everyone be in the kitchen while the pancakes are being made. It's important to joke a little with the cook and to hear the coffee bubbling on the stove and to smell the good heat-containing aroma of the sizzling round patties as they're taken from the griddle and carried to the table. It's important to watch the butter melting, to see the syrup dripping onto the plate. It's important that there be laughter in that kitchen and warmth.

You have to understand pancakes.

ANITA LESLIE ♫ SPINACH PANCAKES Put flour in a bowl. Make a hole in the flour. Add egg, oiled butter. Pour in milk gradually. Beat well with beater. Let stand for at least an hour.

4 ounces plain flour

½ ounce oiled butter

1 egg and 1 yolk

Salt

½ pint milk

Round-leared Savoy Spinach.

Spinach: Cook spinach when well washed in a very little water adding salt to taste. Drain and pass through a fine sieve. Add a little butter and nutmeg. Cool.

264

Béchamel Sauce: Melt butter in a saucepan, add flour and then milk. Cook until it thickens, and add grated cheese.

3 ounces butter or margarine

$\frac{3}{4}$ ounce of flour

About $\frac{1}{2}$ pint milk

2 ounces grated Parmesan cheese

A little mustard

Spinach Pancakes: Put a little butter in a small frying pan. (Have the pancake batter in a jug.) Pour a little batter into the pan, just enough to cover the bottom. When brown, turn, brown the other side and then place it on a sheet of grease-proof paper. Put some cooked spinach on each pancake and roll it up. Place the rolled pancakes in a fireproof dish and cover them with the béchamel sauce. Sprinkle with grated cheese and cook under a grill or in the oven until they are browned. Makes about 1 dozen small pancakes.

MILDRED TOLBERT CREWS ⁂ SOPAIPILLAS (MEXICAN FRIED CAKES)

Sift the flour with salt and baking powder. Cut fat into the flour. Beat eggs and add to the flour mixture. Add enough milk or water to make a medium dough neither stiff nor soft. Let the dough stand for a few minutes, roll out very thin, cut into 1½″ squares and fry in deep fat until brown. Makes about 40 small *sopaipillas.* Eat with cinnamon and sugar.

4 cups flour

1 teaspoon salt

2 teaspoons baking powder

4 tablespoons fat

4 eggs

Water or milk

———— • ————

JOHN LOGAN ⑤ PIZZA The dough may be prepared originally if one has the time. If not, use a hot roll mix, stirring it with a cup of liquid prepared by mixing the enclosed package of yeast with ¾ cup of hot water and adding ¼ cup of olive oil. Let the dough rise. (To hurry this process it may be placed in a 200 degree oven* for half an hour.) Divide the dough, each half being enough for a large pizza the size of a cookie sheet. Roll the dough out very thin after kneading it and let it rise a second time in the pan or on the cookie sheet while preparing the sauce. The following recipe makes the sauce for one pizza, or one half of the prepared dough. (Dough may be refrigerated and kept.)

Anchovy (*Stolephorus encrasicholus*).

Slice one pound mozzarella cheese

Grate one clove of garlic

1 can tomatoes, drained

½ pound sausage and/or

1 can of anchovies

Fresh mushrooms

Sift red pepper lightly over the rolled, thinly-raised dough, add the tomatoes,

*The author puts his in a pilot-lighted clothes dryer.

266

smashed and scattered, the garlic and salt. Arrange the sliced cheese over the surface, then the mushroom and sausage or anchovies. Sprinkle liberally with oregano and finally with grated Parmesan cheese. Cook 20 minutes in a hot oven (450°) or until browned. Eat piping hot.

MARSHALL DAVIS 🐑 CAMPFIRE BISCUITS   This recipe I received from a Montana sheepherder. The only measuring devices are the cupped hand and the thumb and fingers. It works very well and I must say the finished product gives a real sense of accomplishment considering the comparatively rough manner in which it is put together.

It can be baked in any oven that will hold a temperature of from 450 to 500 degrees for about 15 minutes. But the real pleasure comes from baking the biscuits in a reflector oven close to the coals of a medium-sized campfire. To watch these lumps of dough change to a mess of tender, golden-brown biscuits right before your eyes is always an experience. Besides, I always like to believe that a little wood smoke and a few flicks of ashes give a distinct flavor to food.

One cupped handful of flour.

Four fingers and thumb shaped to a point, dip them into a wide-mouthed can of baking powder and take out what you can.

With 3 fingers and thumb, dip into the salt box.

Then, with 2 fingers and thumb, measure out the sugar.

Now, with the index finger dip into the shortening and take out as much as you can get on your finger, up to the first knuckle.

Mix the shortening with the ingredients above — and quickly.

Mix in enough milk or water so that everything holds together, but don't make the dough too wet.

This will make *one portion* — one biscuit about 5 inches wide and 2 inches high or four smaller ones.

Serve with butter and honey.

IRVING STONE ♫ THE PERFECT WRITER'S LUNCHEON I am one of those writers who, as he gets halfway through a long book, decides that there is nothing he can possibly eat that will agree with him. I start out at page 1, line 1, weighing some 170 pounds, and a quarter of a million words later, in seventh draft and ready for the printer, I have come down to 145 pounds. With particularly long books, I get so thin that there is nothing around my hips to hold up my slacks; and, during the last chapters I find it nearly impossible to write sitting down because there is no flesh left to sit on.

As a consequence I have evolved the perfect writer's luncheon, and I have not deviated from it in thirty-five years. My sole and complete lunch consists of an American cheese sandwich on toast and a dish of tea. There are times when the monotony of this lunch is almost unbearable. However, during the last year of the writing of each book, if I attempt to substitute a tongue or beef sandwich, or even a piece of chicken, I am so distressed that I am unable to set down a line during the afternoon.

By a rough estimate, I think I have eaten ten thousand cheese sandwiches during my thirty-five years of concentrated writing. They reached their point of diminishing returns twenty-five years ago, but when one has to make a decision between dietary *ennui* or indigestion — what choice is there?

2 slices of white bread — dull, factory-baked,

full-of-air, unadorned kind.

1 slice pasteurized American cheese — presliced

too thin, be sure no pimento mixed in, too exciting.

Toast bread, lay cheese on one slice, cover with other. On festive, daring occasions put open face in oven for a few minutes to get holiday change.

MARCEL PAGNOL ♫ CROQUE MONSIEUR Between two slices of bread put a slice of *jambon de Parme,* a slice of top quality Swiss cheese and a slice of Roquefort. Broil quickly on both sides. Eat.

DESSERTS

269

VERNON WATKINS ✍ **WELSH CAKES (PICE AR Y MAEN)** Rub the fat into the flour. Add the dry ingredients, then the egg and enough milk to mix into a stiff paste. The dough should be as stiff as that for short pastry. Roll out, cut into rounds and bake on a griddle. These small cakes sprinkled with sugar are irresistible and should be served when children's appetites are appeased by heavier things. This recipe will make about two dozen small cakes.

1 cup flour

½ teaspoon baking powder

¼ cup margarine

¼ cup lard

⅓ cup sugar

¼ cup currants

¼ teaspoon mixed spice

A pinch of salt

1 egg

Milk as needed

RELLA RUDOLPH ✍ **SESAME COOKIES** Add water to ingredients to make a thick dough. Knead well, roll out, cut and cook in moderate oven. Makes four dozen small cookies.

1 cup millet flour

1 cup rye flour

1 cup wheat flour

1 cup chestnut flour

1 tablespoon (heaping) sesame seeds

1 teaspoon sea salt

4 tablespoons sesame oil

1 tablespoon (level) ground cinnamon

ALEXANDRA TOLSTOY ☙ RUSSIAN MINT COOKIES Mix well. Make balls the size of an apricot. Heat stove — 350 degrees. Bake for 12 - 15 minutes till bottom of cookies gets light brown. Keep in closed jar or in a bag in the refrigerator.

The Upper Part of Peppermint (*Mentha piperita*), with flowers.

2 cups sugar

1 cup water

Boil and cool off

Add:

3 tablespoons vegetable oil (any kind)

1 teaspoon baking ammonia (must be ground into powder)

25‑30 drops peppermint oil
5½ cups white flour

ANTONIO MUSIC ♫ FAVETTE ("LITTLE BEANS") Mix together white flour, pieces of butter, two spoons of sugar, two whole eggs, and a little glass of liqueur (Cointreau or Grand Marnier). Knead the dough for a good half hour, until it becomes very soft. Form into some little sticks the diameter of a finger and cut the sticks into small pieces the size of little beans. Then fry in oil or in lard, and dust them with sugar.

White flour

Butter

2 tablespoons of sugar

2 eggs

Small glass of Cointreau or Grand Marnier

Oil or lard

Almond (*Prunus communis*).

ANTONIO MUSIC ♫ TORTION (BIG CAKE) Prepare a beautiful roll of dough, roll it out thinly, and cover it with a mixture of sliced apples, Malaga grapes, pine nuts, little pieces of candied citron, chopped walnuts and almonds. Spread the whole thing with sugar and some pieces of butter. Then roll up the dough so that the stuffing is contained inside. Form the roll into a half-moon, then place it in the oven and bake.

Walnut-tree (*Juglans regia*).

PIERRE SOULAGES ☙ GATEAU A LA BROCHETTE This is a medieval recipe, probably the oldest way of making cake in the world. It is made on a greased brochette or skewer which is turned constantly in front of a fire. Adapted to modern ingredients.

Make a batter with the butter, egg yolks, crushed walnuts and flour, sifting in the other dry ingredients with the flour, adding half of the milk a little at a time. When the flour is damp, beat the batter for 2 minutes. Add the rest of the flour and beat another minute. Put a little on the greased brochette and turn it until the batter holds. Keep adding batter to the brochette, turning it constantly in front of the fire. It will take two hours or more to make a cake 8 inches in diameter. When the cake is done, slide it off the brochette and serve. This is the only cake in the world with the crust *inside*.

½ cup of butter

2 cups of sifted cake flour

1 cup of sugar

2 teaspoons of baking powder

¾ teaspoon salt

5 egg yolks, slightly-beaten

¾ cup of milk

½ cup of crushed walnuts

KAREL APPEL  **CAKE BARBER** Make ten layers of thin pancakes. Between the layers, alternately, place generous amounts of heated apple butter and crisp bacon. Slice like a layer cake and serve steaming hot.

MILDRED TOLBERT CREWS  **TEXAS DOUBLE-DECK PIE** Put a layer of homemade mincemeat (or cook the packaged kind with a little port and water) into an uncooked pie crust. Add a layer of your favorite pumpkin pie custard. Bake in a not-too-hot oven until the custard is set and a light brown.

This is for people who, at holiday time, find it difficult to decide between pumpkin and mince.

Uncooked pie crust

Mincemeat (if packaged kind, also port)

Pumpkin pie custard

ROBERT NEUMANN ✍ MARILLENKNODEL (APRICOT DUMPLINGS)

You should not invite anyone but your very best friends to share this dish with you, first, because it is gorgeous, and secondly, because making lots of it takes some time.

Take two pounds of apricots, small to medium ones if possible, reasonably ripe ones if you can get them. Take out the stones and replace them each with a lump of sugar. Then close the fruit again.

Meanwhile, let five or six medium-sized potatoes boil until they are really soft, then peel them. Put them through a sieve or potato squeezer, add two eggs, a bit of salt, one teaspoonful of olive or nut oil, mix well and add just enough flour to make the dough

Apricot (*Prunus Armeniaca*).

elastic enough to be rolled out flat on a board. Cut the sheet of dough into squares of two or three inches and wrap one of the apricots into each of them. The result: balls of dough with apricots inside. The apricots should be covered completely and the dough should be as thin as possible.

A large pot of water should meanwhile have been brought to a boil. When boiling softly, put in the dumplings with loving care (don't throw in the lot) and let them boil until they come to the surface and stay there. This will take about 15 minutes.

Put a tablespoon of butter into a pan, melt it, add about six ounces of bread crumbs, six ounces of grated nuts, two tablespoonfuls of sugar and heat and stir until the mixture is dark blond.

The cooked dumplings are then rolled in this mixture and they are ready to be served (keep them hot). When on the dish, pour some sugar and melted butter over them.

Drink red wine with them.

Two pounds of apricots, stoned

Lump of sugar for each apricot

Five or six medium potatoes

Two eggs

A bit of salt

One teaspoonful of olive or nut oil

Flour

One tablespoonful of butter, melted

Six ounces of bread crumbs

Six ounces of grated nuts

Two tablespoons of sugar

Additional melted butter and sugar

SAM FRANCIS  SCHAUM TORTE Make two layers of meringue, each to be baked in an 8-inch pan. Mix:

8 stiff-beaten egg whites

$\frac{1}{4}$ teaspoon of cream of tartar

$1\frac{1}{2}$ cups of sugar, added gradually

Beat until the sugar is thoroughly dissolved. Pour half of the mixture into each pan, either greased with butter or lined with wax paper, and bake in a slow oven for about an hour.

Beat 1½ - 2 cups of heavy cream until it is stiff. Wash and slice fresh strawberries or other available fresh fruit.

When the meringue has cooled, place a layer of strawberries on top of one layer of meringue, add about a third of the whipped cream and the second meringue. Top this with the rest of the strawberries and the remaining cream, heaped high and running over the sides of the torte. Serves 4 - 6.

Flowering Branch of *Vanilla planifolia.*
a, the fruit.

JEAN TINGUELY ♫ OMELETTE SOUFFLE DEGONFLE, FLAMBE AU RHUM Mix 3 tablespoons of powdered sugar with the yolks of five eggs. Mix well. Add flavoring to taste — vanilla, lemon or orange peel, grated. Add a teaspoon of grated coconut. Beat the egg whites until stiff. Add ¼ of the whites to the yolk, mix quickly, then add the remaining whites and fold in with the blade of a knife in as few strokes as possible. Place the mixture in a buttered baking dish and dust with powdered sugar. Cook for 20 - 22 minutes in a moderate oven.

    If you wish the soufflé *dégonflé,* wait an hour and a quarter before serving. Otherwise, serve immediately. Add as much rum as desired and *flambé.* Serves 4.

3 tablespoons of powdered sugar

5 eggs (separate yolks from whites)

Vanilla

Lemon or orange peel (grated)

1 teaspoon coconut (grated)

Rum

MARIANNE MOORE ॐ VIAPELLA PUDDING Yes, I cook very conventionally —careful not to invade food with many flavors, even wine. This dessert, I like, given me by a Norwegian cook. I make half the amounts specified:

Lemon Squeezer.

4 eggs, yolks and whites separately beaten

$\frac{1}{2}$ cup of sugar

Juice of one large lemon

Orange juice, half a cup

Water, $\frac{1}{4}$ cup

1 envelope plain Knox gelatine

Soak the gelatine in water for five minutes, then heat in a pan of water till dissolved. Beat the egg yolks with the sugar, add juice and gelatine. Beat the egg whites until stiff and fold in gently. Put in the refrigerator. Before serving add a topping of whipped cream.

———— •◆• ————

ROBEL PARIS 🐌 NEGRE EN CHEMISE In Haiti as in France all ingredients are weighed:

Weigh 4 eggs

Weigh stick of bitter chocolate same amount as eggs

Butter same weight as eggs

Sugar, same weight

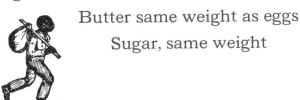

Grate chocolate. Add sugar and 2 tablespoons of strong black coffee. Melt this in a double boiler. Remove from fire. Add butter and mix well. Beat yolks till light color. Add to the above. Beat whites till snowy and add. Pour the mixture into a greased bowl or mold. Chill.

Serve with *Sauce Anglaise:*

4 tablespoons sugar

1 cup evaporated milk

1 stick vanilla

4 egg yolks

Boil the milk. Lower the fire. Add sugar. Remove from fire. Beat egg yolks until thick. Add to hot milk, return to fire and keep stirring and cooking until the sauce is quite thick. Cool. Place in icebox to chill.

DENISE LEVERTOV GOODMAN ℘ A DESSERT This is a dessert I invented. No name attached.

Mix

equal quantities of:

Sour cream

Tart applesauce

Mashed bananas

Add:

Maple syrup to taste

(If you put in too much,

add a little lemon juice)

Top

with: Sliced bananas and walnuts

NOEL BARBER ℘ HOT PINEAPPLE IN BRANDY This recipe I picked up in Malaya during the height of the Communist fighting there. Oddly enough (and I will not give you the recipe for this) I picked it up the same week that I ate a man — or, rather, not a man, but a large steak from one of his legs.

We had been out tracking Chinese Communists — with the aid of Dyak head-hunters — and killed one. There was great merriment in camp that night and a certain amount of delight when some of our native soldiers — as a result (we thought) of a foraging expedition — produced magnificent steaks for dinner. It was not until we had finished dinner that they told us it had been the Chinese we had killed that afternoon.

280

As you know, in the Far East you cannot possibly drink until the sun has gone down — this is the sort of thing we Britishers have been brought up to believe in as strongly as dressing for dinner in the jungle. But nobody can deny that the planters in Malaya, during the Emergency, needed that swift drink in the heat of the noonday sun just as much as they did when dusk had descended.

I was staying with one of the pineapple planters (Malayan pineapples go all over the world, some of them — I regret to say — brazenly labeled "grown in Hawaii") and he produced his brandy pineapple for us. My wife has now made this dish a little more sophisticated. It is very simple.

Pineapple (*Ananas sativa*).

2 large tins of pineapple chunks without the juice
or six small, fresh pineapples, cored and chunked
½ pint of brandy
½ pound of brown sugar
¼ pound of butter

Bake the ingredients in a medium oven in a tightly-covered casserole for about 4 hours. Stir occasionally. It is important that the pineapple does not become too mushy and that there is not too much juice. When the dish is ready the juice from the brandy, sugar and butter should have the consistency of maple syrup. If the mixture is too thin, take the casserole out of the oven and cook it on top of the stove, uncovered, so that it thickens. Serve in individual dishes topped with whipped cream. Or, if you have used fresh pineapples, fill the empty shells about two-thirds full just before serving and top each with whipped cream. Serve hot. The pineapple "hat" can be set on top of each pineapple if you wish. Serves 8.

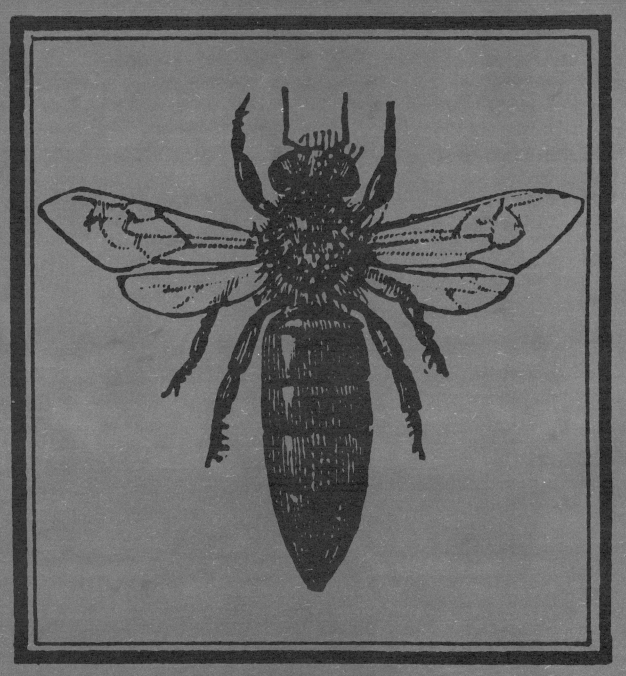

JAMS, JELLIES AND CONFECTIONS

283

ROBERT GRAVES ♫ **SEVILLIAN YELLOW PLUM CONSERVE** Search any cookbook and you are sure to find damsons, greengages and red plums listed in the well-stained jams, marmalades and conserves section; but yellow plums, never. They are too sweet and delicate except as a dessert fruit. We have tried yellow plum with lemon, but that doesn't help; the result is sickly.

One June, our red plum tree failed, and only the yellow plum bore anything. The children were due for their holidays and in Spain, factory-made jams are poor and marmalades worse. But a Seville orange tree was still full of fruit. Summer visitors often steal them, mistaking them for the sweet oranges which are then out of season. I thought: "The very thing!" and, finding the kitchen deserted, made this superlative jam. It is a jam with character and not reminiscent of marmalade because only the orange juice is used, not the peel or pips:

Stone yellow plums and put into a preserving pan with the juice of one large Seville orange for every pound of plums. Bring to a boil. Gradually add ⅔ as much sugar by measure, not allowing the mixture to go off the boil. Stir until the sugar disappears. Boil rapidly. When the jelly stage is reached, about 25 minutes, remove the pan from the fire and cool slightly to stiffen the mixture. Fill jam jars, label, eat.

Juice of Seville oranges

Yellow plums

Sugar

MILDRED TOLBERT CREWS ℌ CHOKECHERRY JELLY Chokecherries are a folk fruit, the wild cherry, producing both food and a medicinal herb. In the old days the Indians dried them for their therapeutic effect upon various ills especially fever. One legend says that tea made from the boiled root will help in cases of anemia. By far the most popular use for chokecherries is jelly. The local (Taos, New Mexico) method is: Pull the clusters of fruit from their stems and wash them. Put them in a pot with an equal amount of quartered greenish apples (chokecherries lack pectin). Cover with cold water and simmer, with a lid on the pot, for several hours until the red color has left the berries. Then strain through a jelly bag. Measure the juice and return it to the pot adding an equal amount of sugar. Boil until the jelly stage is reached and pour up as for any jelly. The jelly will not be clear but cloudy and *muy sabroso.*

Chokecherries and greenish apples
in equal amounts
Sugar in amount equal to the juice

PAUL BOWLES ℌ MAJOUN KEDDANE The Moroccans don't want to divulge their sacred formulas for managing one another. When I ask them, they merely smile and say: "There is food for every purpose, if you know how to prepare it." One Marrakchi was kind enough to give me the following information (which can scarcely be considered a recipe) and I give it to you merely to show you the sort of thing they *are* willing to give. It's called *Beid El Beita F'kerr El Hmar,* and requires three nights to prepare:

Buy an egg. Find a dead donkey, and the first night lodge the egg in its anus. The second night the egg must be put into a mousehole on top of a Moslem tomb. The third night it must be wrapped in a handkerchief and tied around the chest of the person desiring to perform the magic. The following day it must be given for breakfast, prepared in any fashion, to the other individual, who, immediately upon eating it, discovers that the bestower is necessary for his happiness. (Or her happiness; the sex of the two people seems to have nothing to do with the charm's efficacy.)

I keep running into this sort of thing, rather than bonafide cookery secrets. There are, of course, ordinary Moroccan dishes, not designed to produce any particular effect, and they are easy enough to get. Thus, I send the one enclosed true recipe, for *Majoun*. It comes from Fez and has nothing to do with the one Alice Toklas included in her book which was from El Ksar El Kebir.

This food takes time and money to prepare. Fill a cauldron to the two-thirds point with water and put it onto the fire. When it is boiling, add two pounds of fresh *kif (cannabis sativa)** including the stalks. Put in half a pound of unsalted butter. Stir the mixture for eight hours, not continuously, but every few minutes. Take a half pound of wheat grains and run them through a grinder or pound them in a mortar until you have a fairly-coarse powder. Chop walnuts, dates and figs separately, very fine. Pound caraway seeds, aniseed, and part of a nutmeg in a mortar. Mix the chopped nuts and fruit and the spices with a pound of honey.

After the boiling of the *kif* is finished, remove the cauldron from the fire and set it to cool. Scoop all the butter from the top of the vessel. Put a small amount of the wheat powder into a frying pan and stir some of the butter into it, heating the mixture until it becomes brown in color. Continue the operation until all the butter and wheat have been used. Knead the resulting paste into the mass of fruit, nuts, spices and honey. Pack into hermetic glass or metal containers. The jam will last indefinitely. The effect of two teaspoonfuls stays with him who eats it for five or six hours.

Two pounds of fresh *kif*

Half pound unsalted butter

Half pound wheat grain

Editors' note: Kif has the same effect as hashish.

286

Approximately a quarter pound each of dates, dried figs, walnuts

Caraway seed, aniseed (perhaps two ounces together)

Part of a whole nutmeg

One pound of honey

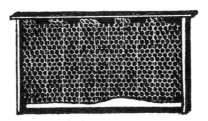

JAMES METCALF 🐝 ALCHEMIST'S TAFFY Sugar was first concentrated from honey. Only later was it boiled from cane as salt from water. Three recipes concerning sugar and confections made from honey were described as medicines in the *Mappae Clavicula*, a book of alchemy written in 1150. Sugar was thought to have a cleansing, solvent and diluent virtue and to remove wateriness of the stomach without corrosion. Issac Judaeus, an Arabian writer of the 10th century, reported that "sugar cleanses the stomach, soothes the lungs, clears the voice, removes coughs and hoarseness, restores humidity, and tempers the sharpness and bitterness of certain aromatics and therefore is of the greatest service in medicine as in electuaries, powders and syrups."

This is probably the oldest recipe in the world for making taffy: Place honey in a vessel, preferably heavy metal. Cook it on a moderate fire for awhile, then remove it and stir while it cools slightly. Return it to the fire and cook and stir some more. Stir it alternately on and off the fire until the honey becomes thick and viscous. Then let it cool. After it is cool, pour it onto a marble slab until it is cold. Then hang it from an iron hook and pull it like taffy, slowly and often. Fold it as you pull it until it becomes very white, then shape it and store it on marble.

VIEIRA DA SILVA ❧ IDEA FOR A TABLE WITH A DIFFERENCE

Roses Farcies

Pick a large, firm, white rose
Cut off the stem at its base
Disclose the center and place it in
the broken heart of a girl.

With the thorns from the stem
Delicately bring together
The broken parts of the heart.

Sprinkle with the tears of the girl
And serve with a separate sauce made
from the blood
Of the wicked man who had broken
her heart.

Flowering Branch of Prairie-rose (*Rosa setigera*).
a, the fruit.

MARK TOBEY ❧ RECIPE FOR A DISH OF NOTHING On a fireless stove and in a state of complete abstraction, place in a well-ungreased pan about two bales of Forest Silence. Remain motionless about 15 minutes. At the boiling point, remove and serve.

FROM THE EDITORS

TAKE THE FRESH BLOOD OF A DRAGON WHICH HAS BEEN MIXED WITH THE BLOOD OF AN ELEPHANT DURING VIOLENT AND MUTUALLY DESTRUCTIVE COMBAT. MIX WITH THE CO-MINGLED BLOOD THE VISCOUS MATTER WHICH EXUDED FROM THE DRAGON DURING THE STRUGGLE.

This is Pliny's recipe and the only formula under the sun or stars fully guaranteed to give the painter a faithful representation of blood. It is said that in Pliny's time indigo blue was mysteriously filtered from the slime of India's rivers and that azure came from beyond the sea like lapis lazuli —exotic, pulverized by magic into pigment. One may imagine artists brewing viridians in rich, mossy glades and for alizarins stirring dark honey with the feather of a flaming drake.

For thousands of years before that first century and the birth of tall tales, and since, painters have been mixing, measuring, blending and brewing. Through all these years, in investigations and experiments with the materials of their expression, artists have developed their own special alchemy. In French slang it is called, aptly, *cuisine*. In today's art vocabulary the word indicates the cookery implicit in the art of painting and—what concerns us—the artists' predilection for it.

As for writers' concern for our subject, it is better to speak of cooking in poetic terms than risk an impious analogy. Consider the gentle assonance of flavors blending into curry, the caesurae which measure the rhythm of a meal, the epigram of a baked Alaska, the singing lyric of a *bouillabaisse*, the polyphonic prose of a mulligatawny stew. The techniques of cooking and of writing are not altogether at variance.

Food forms material for the writer in word and phrase as well as through his own creative simile and metaphor. Food as a slang image is recorded and popularized by the writer. A moldy fig admires Dixieland, while some eggheads dig modern jazz. Noodle or bean is someone's head, and the slang imagery of sex is replete with food terms: tomato, chicken, cheesecake. In French an involved situation is a *salade*. And so on.

The *bon vivants* in the history of literature have written in praise of puddings, onions, sausages, salads, soups and excesses. Sainte-Beuve and Oscar Wilde were notorious gourmands and Ben Jonson once remarked that he who didn't mind his stomach hardly minded anything else.

Both artists and writers have traditionally recognized the poetry and the imagery of a single, simple item of food. Consider the onion. Because of its many layers, its potency, its habitat and its lustre, it is one of the oldest literary and mythological images in the world.

Similarly, the pomegranate, the egg, and the fish—having symbolic connotations—have been used throughout the ages as literary and artistic images. Vlaminck painted lemons, Matisse a plate of oysters, de Chirico bananas, Siqueiros squash. In prose, Charles Lamb found even asparagus gently inspirational, and Edouard Manet glorified a single stalk. It has been said (by the art historian Emile Langui) that modern art grew out of Cézanne's three little apples.

The golden ages of cooking began with the Greeks who were the first to exploit banqueting. They reclined on soft couches and, in homage to Bacchus, ate birds' brains, eggs, wines and spices pounded with fragrant roses cooked in oil. A Greek writer called upon cooks to have a mastery of many arts, first of all a smattering of painting.

The best cooks in Greece were Sicilian and the first cooks in Rome were Greek. During the expansion of their empire, the Romans produced an eclectic cuisine: Jericho dates to be eaten with flamingos or bulbs, African sweet wine cakes which the Romans saturated in milk and covered with honey and pepper, Welsh onions, and cheese from the Alpine regions.

It was the Italians, in the person of Catherine de Médicis, who first brought cookery to France, but the glory of French cuisine rose with Louis XIV. In order to guard the stomach of the Grand Monarch from the grease which he could not digest, Madame de Montaenon invented the "cutlets in curl papers" which bear her name. The king's steward, the Marquis de Béchamel, immortalized that name by his invention of a rich, white sauce. Richelieu invented mayonnaise during the reign of Louis XV and consommé was devised under Louis XVI who considered mastication vulgar. If the Revolution did little for France politically, it spread French cuisine from the court kitchens into the cafés and, subsequently, about the world.

Artists and writers occasionally level indictments against cooking as part of their traditional role in social reform. A not-too-subtle undertone of the response of American artists and writers who have contributed to this book has been in marked protest to those mediocrities of American diet typified by TV dinners, frozen waffles and "sparkling" Burgundy. Ten of the fifteen bread recipes are from Americans, which may imply an understandable reaction against most of American packaged bread. And American artists and writers, as a group of sensibilities, would decry that puritanism indigenous to our culture which adopts a motto spoken by a Molière character, now printed in the Boy Scout Handbook, "Eat to live, don't live to eat."

As creative people involved in and sensitive to the procedures of a culinary aesthetic, are artists and writers *creative* cooks? Alice B. Toklas snorts at the idea of a creative cook. There are, she says, seldom new recipes. It has been our observation that most persons who are dedicated to a life of creative activity and who cook, do so in the same spirit in which they paint, sculpt or write. If the love of beauty is taste (as Emerson thought) and creative persons, by virtue of their special gifts, can communicate this taste—for food, for gardening, for any activity which plays a role in their lives—that is aesthetic communication and, as such, creative. For that reason we feel this book is a pertinent expression of the continuity or unity of creativity.

. We have encouraged the touch of caprice in this collection. One can find remnants of the pathetic fallacy as well. There are echoes of the statement which the Pudding made to Alice—"What impertinence! I wonder how you would like it if I were to cut a slice out of *you,* you creature."

Measurements are not always explicit, ingredients are occasionally interchangeable, and the length of cooking time is sometimes regarded as an act of pure intuition. The number of servings for several recipes is solely dependent on the size of the fish or the pot, and we decided that a wineglassful is a wineglassful, not to be measured in cups. Likewise, a handful is just that.

The genesis of a book of this nature seems all too obvious when the book is an accomplished fact. But the book would never have been realized without a person of energy and ideas who was able to foresee its potentialities. This is William H. Ryan, the publisher of Contact Editions, who had the idea and believed the book was possible. Miss Kay Boyle of Rowayton, Connecticut, and Mme. Jacqueline Ballance of Paris have been helpful in enlisting the interest of artists and writers; Paul Turner, Irving Stone, Martin Gang, Richard Armour of Los Angeles, Christopher Amunssen of New York City and Charles Potts of Salisbury, Maryland, gave generously of their professional advice. Joe Barry of Paris and the New York *Post* was of assistance to Miss Alice B. Toklas.

Reprint rights were obtained from Prentice-Hall for the Elise Cavanna recipes which appear in *Gourmet Cookery for a Low-Fat Diet* by Elise Cavanna and James Welton, revised edition, 1961; and from Doubleday and Company for the Frances Parkinson Keyes recipe from *The Frances Parkinson Keyes Cookbook,* 1955.

CONTRIBUTORS

LEON D. ADAMS ℌ is a resident of Sausalito, California. He helped found the Wine Institute and is the author of *The Commonsense Book of Wine* and *Striped Bass Fishing*. Page 59.

CONRAD AIKEN ℌ has published several volumes of collected poems. His latest work is *The Collected Short Stories of Conrad Aiken*. Page 14.

MARY HOOVER AIKEN ℌ is a painter who has done portraits of T. S. Eliot, St. John Perse and Allen Tate. She has two pictures hanging at the Metropolitan Museum of Art. She lives in Brewster, Massachusetts with her husband, Conrad. Page 65.

JEAN AMES ℌ designs tapestries which are woven for her by the world-renowned craftsmen at Aubusson in France. She teaches at Scripps College in Claremont, California. Page 11.

CHARLES ANGOFF ℌ was born in Minsk, Russia in 1902. He has published some 30 works of fiction, history and criticism. Page 211.

KAREL APPEL ℌ is a Dutch artist and winner (1960) of the Guggenheim International Award in Painting. He has lived since 1948 in Paris, where in his very early years he often traded a painting for a meal, two paintings for a meal with meat. Pages 150, 174, 274.

HERBERT ASBURY ℌ wrote the classic *Gangs of New York* and *The Barbary Coast*. Page 160.

LOUIS AUCHINCLOSS ℌ was born in New York in 1917. He currently practices law there. His most recent book is *The House of Five Talents*. Pages 169, 191.

MUDITE AUSTRINA ℌ owes her lyric name to a Latvian origin. Intrepid journalist, tireless traveller and unpublished poet, Miss Austrina has just returned from the high sierras of Peru. She lives in Sausalito, California. Page 210.

NOEL BARBER ℌ of the *Daily Mail*, London, was the first Briton to reach the South Pole since Scott in 1912. He now lives with his wife and two children on the edge of the Thames, in a studio once occupied by the English painter J. M. W. Turner. Pages 30, 280.

ROGER BARR ℌ is an American painter resident in Paris. He is married to Beryl Barr, co-editor of *The Artists' and Writers' Cookbook*. Page 19.

SYBILLE BEDFORD ℌ who was born in Germany, now lives in England. Her best-known work is the novel, *A Legacy*. Page 2.

NATHANIEL BENCHLEY ⑤ writes for *The New Yorker* and has published several books. He is a resident of New York. Page 123.

JOHN BERRY ⑤ won the Macmillan Fiction Prize in 1959 with *Krishna Fluting*. He lives in Santa Monica, California with his wife, Ynez Johnston. Page 84.

STREETER BLAIR ⑤ comes from the Midwest. He is a primitive painter and lives in a white frame house in Beverly Hills where he paints, reads Proust and tells stories to his grandchildren. Page 257.

PAUL BOWLES ⑤ was born in New York and now resides in Tangier. His novels include *The Sheltering Sky* and *The Spider's House*. Page 285.

KAY BOYLE ⑤ was born in Minnesota, has lived in France, England and Austria, and now resides in Connecticut. Author of over twenty books, her latest is *Generation Without Farewell*. Pages 122, 222.

MALCOLM BRADBURY ⑤ was born in Sheffield, England in 1932. *Eating People is Wrong* is one of his recent books. Page 248.

RICHARD EMIL BRAUN ⑤ writes, "Since first hearing and reading *Cyrano de Bergerac,* I have planned to do a sequence of recipes, contriving the metric to suit the flavor." He is a poet and lives now in Texas. Pages 22, 205, 211, 216.

JAMES BROOKS ⑤ one of the original participants in the American Abstract-Expressionist movement, grew up in various parts of the West. He now lives in New York. Pages 256, 257.

VAN WYCK BROOKS ⑤ is one of America's oldest and finest deans of letters. Born in New Jersey, he lives and writes in Bridgewater, Connecticut. Page 31.

PEARL BUCK ⑤ won the Nobel Prize for Literature in 1938. She has just finished producing a film from her short story, *The Big Wave*. Page 175.

JACKSON BURGESS ⑤ has just had a new novel published, *The Atrocity*. Georgia-born, he has been in Northern California for two years. Page 208.

SAMUEL BURI ⑤ is a young Swiss painter, born and educated in Basel, now living in Paris. Page 13.

NIVEN BUSCH ⑤ A past editor of *Time* and *The New Yorker,* he was born in New York, came to Hollywood to write motion pictures such as *Duel in the Sun*. He lives with his two sons on a ranch in San Benito, California. Page 136.

ERSKINE CALDWELL ℌ is a very famous writer. Page 92.

ELISE CAVANNA ℌ is a painter, an expert cook, an inveterate letter writer and a veteran movie actress. She smokes a pipe while painting every morning and lives in Los Angeles. Pages 25, 67, 246.

CESAR'S ℌ sculpture is welded metal made from nuts, bolts, bits of tubing, and once, from two automobiles pressed into cubes. He lives and works in Paris. Page 194.

LYNN CHADWICK ℌ is one of Britain's most important sculptors. He lives in a modernized medieval castle in Gloucestershire with his wife and two small daughters. Pages 58, 194.

EMILE COMPARD ℌ was born in Paris in 1900. He was a friend of Bonnard and studied with the Cubists during the 1920's. Page 23.

EVAN S. CONNELL, JR. ℌ is from Kansas City, but now lives in San Francisco. He is the author of *Mrs. Bridge* and two other books. He is an editor of *Contact* magazine. Page 105.

ANYA SETON CHASE ℌ "My tastes are eclectic and I use recipes from all nations. I do not serve such national delicacies as Mexican fried Maguey worms, or the Near East's boiled sheep eyes. But I enjoy them in their native heath." She writes historical novels. Page 170.

CORNEILLE ℌ a Dutch painter, lives in Paris where he and his wife, also Dutch, often prepare dishes typical of the Hintelopen region of Holland. Pages 97, 174.

DAVID CORNEL DeJONG ℌ has published 9 novels, 3 collections of short stories, 4 volumes of poetry, 5 children's books, and more. Netherlands born, he lives in Rhode Island. Page 100.

A. COSTA ℌ Parisian born painter, Greek citizen, lives in London and is currently at work on a book about Morocco. Page 236.

HAROLD COUSINS ℌ is an American sculptor who has lived in Paris since 1949. Pages 99, 190.

MILDRED TOLBERT CREWS ℌ is from Texas and now lives in Taos, New Mexico. She is a journalist and photographer and is married to the poet, Judson Crews. Pages 265, 274, 285.

RUPERT CROFT-COOKE ℌ was born in England, now lives in Tangier. He is a free-lance writer, author of *The Gardens of Camelot* and other books. Page 144.

CARESSE CROSBY ⚜ has published *Cross of Gold, Painted Shores* and *The Stranger*. Page 69.

PIERRE DANINOS ⚜ born in 1913, is a French novelist and journalist best known perhaps for his *Notebooks of Major Thompson* which has sold more than a million copies. He carefully establishes that he is a humorist, not a comedian. Page 96.

GWEN DAVENPORT ⚜ has published, among other books, *Belvedere*, filmed as "Sitting Pretty." Page 251.

MARSHALL DAVIS ⚜ does free-lance illustration and reportage. He lives with his Swedish-born wife, who is also a painter, and their son in South Norwalk, Connecticut. Page 267.

BEAUFORD DELANEY ⚜ is an American Negro painter, born in Knoxville, Tennessee, in 1901. He now lives in the Auvergne region of France. Page 224.

ARTHUR DESHAIES ⚜ an American artist of French parentage, recently won a Guggenheim Fellowship for his printmaking. He describes himself as "Thoreauic, red-bearded and pipe-smoking." Pages 62, 108, 243.

ISAK DINESEN ⚜ is Denmark's most famous author. She is the Baroness Blixen and lives on the seacoast north of Copenhagen. Page 78.

DONALD DOWNES' ⚜ *Orders to Kill* is based on his experience in espionage during World War II. His most recent novel is *The Easter Dinner*. Page 157.

MARCEL DUCHAMP ⚜ voluntarily terminated his artistic career in 1925 and now lives in New York City. The Duchamp painting best-known to the general public, *Nude Descending a Staircase,* hangs in the Philadelphia Museum of Art. Page 138.

NATALIA DUMITRESCO ⚜ is a Roumanian painter who lives in Paris. She has traveled in Holland, Italy and Spain and once, with her husband, the painter Alexandre Istrati, went by Greyhound bus from New York to California. Pages 106, 194.

LAWRENCE DURRELL ⚜ lives in the south of France, "where red wine costs a shilling a litre, cigarettes are cheap and sunshine unrationed." His *Alexandria Quartet* was a recent sensation. Pages 4, 38.

MAX EASTMAN ⚜ was born in western New York state in 1883. A poet, essayist, and teacher, he has recently published *Poems of 5 Decades*. Page 13.

WALTER EDMONDS ⚜ is an American novelist best known for his *Drums Along the Mohawk*. He was born in 1903, lives in New England, where, in Proustian fashion, he sleeps in the room in which he was born. Page 245.

ROBERT ELLIS ⚘ a painter and the Curator of Education at the Pasadena Museum of Art, spent a year in Paris and has traveled extensively in Europe. Page 139.

EMLEN ETTING ⚘ was born in Philadelphia and studied at Harvard and in Paris. He illustrated his own translation of Paul Valéry's *Graveyard by the Sea* and the English version of *Amerika* by Franz Kafka. Page 37.

ENID FOSTER ⚘ was born in San Francisco in 1895 and now lives in Sausalito. She began her career in sculpture but turned to painting and graphics. Pages 61, 172.

SAM FRANCIS ⚘ is one of the most highly-regarded American painters in Europe. He was born in San Mateo, California and now lives in Paris. Pages 58, 138, 276.

FREDERICK FRANCK ⚘ is a Holland-born artist, writer, and doctor. He was introduced to crocodile eating at the hospital of Dr. Albert Schweitzer where he has worked repeatedly. Pages 119, 120.

HELEN FRANKENTHALER ⚘ is a young American painter living in New York. She is married to Robert Motherwell. Page 141.

ELIZABETH FRINK ⚘ is a young English sculptress. Page 107.

TERRY FROST ⚘ is an English painter living and working in Cornwall. He began painting as a prisoner of war in Germany. Page 220.

ILSE GETZ ⚘ is an American painter living in Paris. She works principally in the medium of collage and is married to the painter Manoucher Yektai. Page 98.

HARRY GOLDEN ⚘ lives in a high-porched ante-bellum home in Charlotte, North Carolina where he puts out the newspaper, *The Carolina Israelite*. Page 143.

NATHALIE GONCHAROVA ⚘ born in Russia in 1881, has lived in Paris since 1914. She designs costumes and sets for the Diaghilev ballets. Page 33.

DENISE LEVERTOV GOODMAN ⚘ born in London in 1923 of Russian-Welsh descent, was educated at home, studied ballet, and eventually became a poet. She now lives in New York and is married to the writer, Mitchell Goodman. Page 280.

RAYMOND GRANDJEAN ⚘ is a French painter, born in Lyon. Page 107.

ROBERT GRAVES ⚘ has lived on Majorca for years. He was born in 1895 at Wimbleton. He is the author of a prodigious number of volumes. Page 284.

NANCY HALE ⚘ Unlike many women, her hobby is cooking and writing is her full-time job. She lives in Charlottesville, Virginia. Page 34.

S. I. HAYAKAWA ℬ teaches at San Francisco State College. He was born in Vancouver, British Columbia, in 1906. His best-known work is *Language in Thought and Action*. He is a general semanticist. Page 135.

STANLEY WILLIAM HAYTER ℬ internationally famous printmaker, has been awarded the Légion d'honneur and a decoration from Queen Elizabeth. Page 22.

LILLIAN HELLMAN ℬ grew up in New Orleans and New York. Among her plays are *Watch on the Rhine* and *The Autumn Garden*. Page 68.

HILAIRE HILER ℬ is a painter and author now living in Paris. Page 122.

DEREK HILL ℬ packs provisions into a boat each summer and sails to Tory Island off the coast of Ireland, where he paints for a month in primitive conditions. Page 56.

ROBERT HILLYER ℬ is a well-known poet and man of letters. Page 47.

PHILIP HIQUILY ℬ is a Parisian sculptor. He won the Paris Biennial Critics' Award in 1959. Pages 63, 78, 138.

PHILIP HOSIASSON ℬ a Russian painter, is now a French citizen. Page 140.

EVAN HUNTER ℬ a native of New York, has written more than 100 short stories and articles besides his well-known *Blackboard Jungle*. Page 262.

ALEXANDRE ISTRATI ℬ went to Paris in 1947 from his home in Roumania. He is a painter married to the painter Natalia Dumitresco. Page 255.

BURL IVES ℬ is a well-known author in the oral tradition. Page 196.

PAUL JENKINS ℬ an American painter, was born in Kansas City and has divided his time between New York and Paris since 1953. Page 66.

RALPH JOHNSON ℬ is an American painter living in Northern California. He once had a job as a hod carrier for an old Danish bricklayer who liked to cook. Page 17.

JAMES JONES ℬ wrote *From Here to Eternity*. Page 195.

MERVIN JULES ℬ is a professor of art at Smith College. Pages 32, 40, 160, 233.

MATSUMI KANEMITSU ℬ was born in Utah in 1922. He lived in Japan for 18 years, fought with the nisei battalion in Italy in World War II. He now lives in New York. He is a painter and printmaker. Pages 38, 142.

LENN KANENSON ℬ was born in Pennsylvania in 1920. He lives in Muir Beach, California and is currently painting in Europe. Page 13.

NORMAN KANTER 〽 is an American painter living in New York. He spent a year in France on a Fulbright Fellowship, and now lives in a loft on the lower West Side where he cooks on a two-burner gas stove. Page 176.

ALEX KARMEL 〽 a Fulbright scholar, had written and discarded three other novels before publication of *Maryann*. He lives in New York. Pages 93, 109.

JOHN KEATS 〽 writes, "Naturally I like to cook, and it's a damned good thing that I do, because my wife went to Smith." They live part of the year on an island in the St. Lawrence. Pages 8, 52, 112.

CALVIN KENTFIELD 〽 a founding editor of *Contact,* has a new novel, as yet untitled, due in March, 1962. Pages 149, 177.

FRANCES PARKINSON KEYES 〽 has written many popular novels. Page 240.

JOHN KNOWLES' 〽 novel, *A Separate Peace*, won the first Faulkner Foundation award. He lives in Brooklyn. Page 252.

ROGER KUNTZ 〽 plays the trumpet, tells dirty jokes, and paints leisurely in the tradition of an Impressionist. Page 60.

MICHEL LARIONOV 〽 was one of the earliest abstract painters. He was born in Odessa and designed for Diaghilev's ballet for many years. Pages 20, 168.

C. Y. LEE 〽 is the author of several novels, the best-known being *The Flower Drum Song*. He was born in China and lives in San Francisco. Page 75.

HARPER LEE 〽 launched her literary career in 1961 by writing the Pulitzer Prize-winning first novel, *To Kill a Mockingbird*. Page 251.

ANITA LESLIE 〽 daughter of Sir Shane Leslie, is the author of *The Fabulous Leonard Jerome*. Page 264.

SIR SHANE LESLIE 〽 an Irish writer, is a first cousin of Winston Churchill. He has written biographies, memoirs and short stories. Page 254.

JOHN LEVEE 〽 an American painter, is one of the younger painters of the Ecole de Paris. Pages 167, 212.

JACQUES LIPCHITZ 〽 the sculptor, was born in Lithuania in 1891, went to Paris where he was a friend of Diego Rivera, Picasso, and Juan Gris, and since World War II has settled permanently near New York. Page 161.

JOHN LOGAN 〽 has published poetry and stories in many magazines. He is an associate professor at Notre Dame University and has nine children. Page 266.

JERRE MANGIONE ℘ is a writer of Sicilian origin. "My father is a genius of a pastry cook; his speciality is *connalla,* a delicacy to which I devoted half a chapter in my first book, *Mount Allegro.*" He lives in Philadelphia. Page 238.

MONIKA MANN ℘ the daughter of Thomas Mann, has published about 100 short stories and two novels. She lives in Capri. Page 5.

HARRISON McINTOSH ℘ has taught pottery making and worked as a ceramic designer in Los Angeles. Page 244.

JAMES MERRILL ℘ is a young poet, novelist, playwright, and benefactor of artists. Page 128.

JAMES METCALF ℘ is an American sculptor living in Paris. He has made a study of ancient methods of metal-working. Page 287.

JAMES MICHENER ℘ considers himself an expert on two countries only — Mexico and Scotland, about which he has never written a word. Page 134.

MICHEL MISHORIT ℘ is a young Israeli painter living in New York with a husband and a collection of paintings. Pages 24, 209.

PIERRE MONOSIET ℘ a painter, is director of Le Centre d'Art in Haiti. Page 162.

DOUGLAS MOORE ℘ author of books on music, won the Pulitzer prize in 1951 for his opera, *Giants in the Earth.* His latest opera is *The Wings of the Dove.* Page 204.

MARIANNE MOORE ℘ is one of the world's greatest poets, letter-writers and women-about-zoos. Page 278.

ANTONIO MUSIC ℘ has studios in both Paris and Venice. This well-known Italian painter favors the old Venetian cuisine. Page 272.

JOAN NEUHOF ℘ is an American sculptress now living in Paris. Pages 115, 237.

ROBERT NEUMANN ℘ is the English author of *By the Waters of Babylon* and other books. He currently lives in Switzerland. Page 275.

HIDETAKA OHNO ℘ lives in southern Japan where he experiments with burlap forms resting on tinted canvases. Page 246.

RICHARD OLNEY ℘ studied at the University of Iowa and the Brooklyn Museum School, and paints now in Paris. Page 47.

ROBERT OSBORN ℘ began as a painter and did not develop his genius for graphic satire until he was 42 when he was assigned to the creation of safety posters in the Navy. His books include *War is No Damn Good* and *The Vulgarians.* Page 17.

MARCEL PAGNOL ♫ is a member of the Académie Francaise. Originally a playwright, since 1932 he has devoted himself almost entirely to writing for films. Best-known of his films is the *Marius* trilogy. Page 268.

ROBEL PARIS ♫ spent six years in Haiti teaching silk screen printing and learning voodoo. She lives and works in San Francisco. Page 279.

PAT PASLOV ♫ lives and paints in New York. Page 60.

KENNETH PATCHEN ♫ poet and novelist, lives near San Francisco. Among his books are the *Journal of Albion Moonlight* and *Hurrah for Anything*. Page 216.

SIDNEY PETERSON ♫ was director of the Museum of Modern Art's TV project, then wrote scenarios for UPA and Walt Disney in Hollywood. This year Contact Editions published his first novel *A Fly in the Pigment*. Page 117.

KATHERINE ANNE PORTER'S ♫ famous unfinished novel, *Ship of Fools*, is finished and will be published in March, 1962. Page 45.

ANTHONY POWELL ♫ is writing a series of linked novels called *The Music of Time*. He lives in the English countryside. Page 186.

DACHINE RAINER ♫ has lived for the last 16 years in a log cabin in Bearsville, New York where she writes poetry and novels. Page 180.

MAN RAY ♫ founded the New York school of Dadaism in 1917. Also known as a photographer, from 1940 to 1951 he produced surrealistic films in Hollywood. He now lives in Paris. Page 5.

KRISHNA REDDY ♫ is an Indian printmaker who lives and works in Paris as assistant director of Atelier 17, the school-workshop of Stanley William Hayter. Page 184.

MILTON RESNICK ♫ lives and paints in New York. Page 141.

MAURICE REY ♫ began to paint non-figuratively after a trip to the Far East in 1952. He lives in France. Page 99.

BERTON ROUECHE ♫ for years has been *The New Yorker's* relentless medical sleuth. Among his articles subsequently published in book form are *Incurable Wound, The Delectable Mountains,* and *Neutral Spirit.* Page 43.

RELLA RUDOLPH ♫ constructs geometric aluminum compositions which she exhibits in Paris and elsewhere. Pages 261, 270.

FELIX RUVULO ♫ is a painter and professor of art at the University of California in Berkeley. Pages 26, 80, 218, 219.

JOHN SACCARO ℐ is an abstract painter living in San Francisco. Page 202.

PIERRE SCHNEIDER ℐ writes French poetry and is a Paris correspondent for several art publications, notably *Art News* and *Art International*. Page 104.

MARY SCOTT ℐ exhibits her bronzes in London and New York. She is married to the English painter, William Scott. Page 224.

ALLAN SEAGER ℐ teaches at the University of Michigan. His novels include *The Death of Anger* and *Amos Berry*. Page 16.

SUEO SERISAWA ℐ came to the United States from Japan as a young boy. He now lives and paints in Los Angeles. Page 73.

CLANCY SIGAL ℐ is thirty-five, lives in London and regularly contributes to the *Observer*. He is the author of the novel, *Weekend in Dinlock*. Page 18.

GEORGES SIMENON ℐ has written over 170 novels which have been translated into 28 languages. Thirty-five of his books have been made into movies. His Inspector Maigret is one of the best-known characters in detective fiction. Page 166.

UPTON SINCLAIR ℐ has devoted his life to experimental causes from muckraking to the controversial backing of Sergei Eisenstein. Among his many novels are *The Jungle*, the Pulitzer Prize-winning *Dragon's Teeth*, and an autobiography. Page 228.

ARNOLD SINGER ℐ is a young New York painter. Page 204.

VELTA SNICKERE ℐ is a Latvian poet living in London. Page 27.

KURT SONDERBORG ℐ studied painting in Germany. He lives in New York and Paris. Page 41.

PIERRE SOULAGES ℐ a native of the Auvergne region of France, acknowledges an influence on his work of the prehistoric caves in the Dordogne Valley, principally Lascaux. Pages 108, 117, 176, 273.

RALPH STACKPOLE ℐ an American sculptor now living in France, was originally from San Francisco where his murals can be seen in Coit Tower. Pages 19, 243.

MAX STEELE ℐ was awarded the Harper prize of $10,000 for his first novel *Debby*. He lives and writes in San Francisco. Page 261.

GWEN STONE ℐ paints large abstract canvases in a long narrow studio near San Francisco. Pages 24, 124.

IRVING STONE ⑤ "After having written short stories and one-act plays for several years, I encountered, while in Europe in 1930, the life and works of Vincent Van Gogh; 3 years later *Lust for Life* emerged and I suddenly found myself a biographer." Page 268.

WILLIAM STYRON ⑤ wrote *Lie Down in Darkness, The Long March,* and most recently *Set This House on Fire.* Born in Virginia, he now lives in Connecticut. Page 87.

KUMI SUGAI ⑤ is a Japanese painter now living in Paris. Page 72.

HARVEY SWADOS' ⑤ books include *False Coin, On the Line, Out Went the Candle,* and *Nights in the Gardens of Brooklyn.* He has lived in France, Mexico, and many parts of the United States. Page 203.

SHU TANAKA ⑤ was born and educated in Tokyo, but has lived and painted in Paris since 1954. Page 127.

JEAN TINGUELY ⑤ is the Swiss sculptor probably best known as the creator of a machine 24 feet high entitled *Homage to New York* which destroyed itself in half-an-hour in the garden of the Museum of Modern Art in 1959. Page 277.

MARK TOBEY ⑤ spent much of his life in Seattle, Washington. He has traveled throughout the world and now lives and paints in Switzerland. Page 288.

ALEXANDRA TOLSTOY ⑤ is the authoritative biographer of her father, and has also published her own account *I Worked for the Soviets.* She now lives in New York and is curator of the Tolstoy Museum. Page 271.

LOUIS UNTERMEYER ⑤ once said, "Culture is my excuse; cookery is my central passion." Nevertheless he has written and collected some 70 volumes of prose, poetry, short stories, travel books, essays and critical anthologies. Page 126.

JEAN VARDA ⑤ born in Greece, now lives on a barge in Sausalito, California, where he constructs his brightly-colored collages. Pages 36, 64, 78.

EDGARD VARESE ⑤ His first orchestral work to be performed was titled *Bourgogne* in honor of the famous French dish. He lives in Paris. Page 132.

HELENE VIEIRA DA SILVA ⑤ devised fanciful recipes which share the magic and illusory quality of her paintings. A native of Portugal, she now lives in Paris. Page 288.

PETER VIERECK ⑤ now a professor of modern history at Mount Holyoke College, won the Pulitzer Prize in 1949 for his first book of poems. Pages 200, 201.

IRA WALLACH ⑤ is perhaps best known for his collection of literary satires, *Hopalong Freud.* He lives in Brooklyn. Pages 11, 28.

BARNEY WAN ☖ original art director for *Contact*, was born in China and lives at present in London. He is known for his drawings and watercolors as well as his commercial work. Pages 72, 232.

FRANKLIN WATKINS ☖ is a Philadelphia painter well-known for his portraits. Page 196.

VERNON WATKINS ☖ writes poetry in Wales, where he also works for a Lloyds Bank. Pages 37, 79, 252, 270.

EPHREM WEITZMAN ☖ is a young stained-glass window designer who lives and works in New York. Pages 33, 232.

ANTHONY WEST ☖ "fell in love with America through the eye..." and left the old England for the New. A frequent contributor to *The New Yorker,* he has also written *The Vintage* and *Principles and Persuasions.* Pages 3, 40, 154, 158, 253.

WILLIAM L. WHITE ☖ is publisher and editor of the *Emporia Gazette,* following in the footsteps of his father William Allen White. He was a war correspondent for *Life* and wrote the best-selling book *They Were Expendable.* Page 241.

RICHARD WILBUR ☖ lives and teaches in Oregon, and is a frequent contributor to *The New Yorker* and *The Atlantic.* His collection of poems *Things of This World* was awarded the Pulitzer Prize in 1957. Page 217.

SLOAN WILSON ☖ created the Madison Avenue archetype, *The Man In The Grey Flannel Suit,* and lives in New England. Other novels include *A Summer Place* and *A Sense of Values.* Page 110.

LIN YUTANG ☖ "I love debates on theology and adore all mountains," says the China-born author, translator, satirist and philosopher. Some of his books are *The Importance of Living, The Importance of Understanding* and *Gay Genius.* Page 80.

MANOUCHER YEKTAI ☖ is a Persian painter living in Paris. Pages 27, 232.

JACK ZAJAC ☖ is perhaps best known for a series of bronze goats, each with a stake driven through its belly, representing, says the artist, man as he sins against himself. He lives in California with his wife, his mother and his violin. Page 81.